INSIGHT GUIDES

EXPLORE

BOSTON

created 08/27/19 *UPDATED & CREATED 8-27-2019* *2/13/23*

⊙ Walking Eye App

YOUR FREE EBOOK AVAILABLE THROUGH THE WALKING EYE APP

Your guide now includes a free eBook to your chosen destination, for the same great price as before. Simply download the Walking Eye App from the App Store or Google Play to access your free eBook.

HOW THE WALKING EYE APP WORKS

Through the Walking Eye App, you can purchase a range of eBooks and destination content. However, when you buy this book, you can download the corresponding eBook for free. Just see below in the grey panel where to find your free content and then scan the QR code at the bottom of this page.

Destinations: Download essential destination content featuring recommended sights and attractions, restaurants, hotels and an A–Z of practical information, all available for purchase.

Ships: Interested in ship reviews? Find independent reviews of river and ocean ships in this section, all available for purchase.

eBooks: You can download your free accompanying digital version of this guide here. You will also find a whole range of other eBooks, all available for purchase.

Free access to travel-related blog articles about different destinations, updated on a daily basis.

HOW THE EBOOKS WORK

The eBooks are provided in EPUB file format. Please note that you will need an eBook reader installed on your device to open the file. Many devices come with this as standard, but you may still need to install one manually from Google Play.

The eBook content is identical to the content in the printed guide.

HOW TO DOWNLOAD THE WALKING EYE APP

1. Download the Walking Eye App from the App Store or Google Play.
2. Open the app and select the scanning function from the main menu.
3. Scan the QR code on this page – you will then be asked a security question to verify ownership of the book.
4. Once this has been verified, you will see your eBook in the purchased ebook section, where you will be able to download it.

Other destination apps and eBooks are available for purchase separately or are free with the purchase of the Insight Guide book.

CONTENTS

ARCHITECTURE

Beacon Hill (Route 5), Back Bay (Route 6), and the South End (Route 9) feature grand architecture from the 17th to early 20th centuries. The Institute of Contemporary Art at Fort Point (Route 10) is a fantastic 21st-century addition.

RECOMMENDED ROUTES FOR...

ART ENTHUSIASTS

If you love art, don't miss the Museum of Fine Arts and Isabella Stewart Gardner Museum (Route 8), or visit Salem's Peabody Essex Museum (Route 12), Cape Ann's art colonies (Route 13), or Provincetown's galleries (Route 16).

CHILDREN

The Aquarium and the Children's Museum (Route 10) are great for the little ones, as is the Museum of Science (Route 4). Don't forget the USS Constitution (Route 2) and the Plimoth Plantation (Route 15) either.

FOOD AND WINE

Dine out in either the North End (Route 2) or South End (Route 9) and your stomach will be very happy. Harvard Square (Route 3) is also a fine place to eat, as is Newbury Street in Back Bay (Route 6).

PARKS AND GARDENS

Boston's Emerald Necklace of parks and gardens extends from the Common (Route 1) through the Public Garden (Route 5) and Commonwealth Avenue's central boulevard (Route 6) to the Back Bay Fens (Route 7).

REVOLUTIONARY BOSTON

Follow the Freedom Trail of revolutionary sites through Downtown (Route 1), North End and Charlestown (Route 2), then head out of town to follow the 'Battle Road' between Lexington and Concord (Route 14).

SCIENCE AND TECHNOLOGY

The Museum of Science and the MIT Museum and campus (Route 4) have outstanding boffin appeal, as do Harvard's Peabody Museum and Museum of Natural History (Route 3).

WATERSIDE VIEWS

You are seldom far from water in Boston, be it the Charles River (Route 4) or Boston Harbor (Routes 2 and 10). To get out on the water, take a ferry to the Harbor Islands (Route 11) or Provincetown, Cape Cod (Route 16).

INTRODUCTION

An introduction to Boston's geography, customs and culture, plus illuminating background information on cuisine, history and what to do when you're there.

An aerial view of Boston's old brownstones

EXPLORE BOSTON

Boston is considered the most 'European' of American cities – hardly surprising given its British Colonial roots. But this is also the birthplace of the country's independence, and home to some of its most illustrious Ivy League institutions.

Boston is small (population 667,137 as of 2016) and compact (48.5 sq. miles/125 sq. km), making it an ideal city for discovering on foot. It may only be the 22nd-largest city in the US in size, but in historical legacy Boston is huge. Among the lofty phrases coined to describe the city are the 'Cradle of Liberty', the 'Athens of America', and 'the Hub of the Universe' (a variant of the latter was first used by one of Boston's greatest literary sons Oliver Wendell Holmes to describe the State House).

A rich heritage

Many visitors come here to walk in the footsteps of the Founding Fathers and soak up the Old World atmosphere that nurtured some of America's most gifted artistic, mercantile, and political talents, including the poet Henry Wadsworth Longfellow (1807–82), the artist John Singer Sargent (1856–1925), and President John F. Kennedy (1917–63). Boston plays up this rich heritage in projects such as the Freedom Trail, the Black Heritage Trail, and the Battle Road Trail between Lexington and Concord. That many historical monuments and sites have been preserved as part of the fabric of the city is a large part of Boston's appeal. The US National Parks Service records 186 National Historic Landmarks in the state of Massachusetts; only New York State beats it with 261. A good proportion of these sites are found in the Boston city area and surrounding towns such as Concord, Lexington, Plymouth, Provincetown, and Salem.

HARBOR CITY

Boston's fortunes first came from its harbor, and this was a pivotal part of the city up until the early 20th century. With the end of the Big Dig and the city's promotion of the HarborWalk route, attention is now flowing back to the long-neglected seashore. From May to mid-October you can take public ferries out to some of the 34 islands that are one of the city's biggest, yet least-known, natural assets. Another is its Emerald Necklace of parks and gardens – Boston is one of America's greenest cities. The Emerald Necklace – a corridor of interlinked parklands and gardens stretching for 7 miles (11km) from Boston Common to Franklin Park – was designed by Frederick Law Olmsted (1822–1903). He also con-

View of Back Bay, Charles River, and Longfellow Bridge

ceived the beautiful Esplanade park that hugs the south bank of the Charles River, but which was not built until the 1930s, and New York's Central Park.

SPLIT PERSONALITY

Walking in Boston is often a necessity due to the traffic chaos (an old joke has it, 'Shall we walk or do we have time to take a cab?'), but it is also a pleasure as walking enables one to savor the strange contradictions of this untypical town. The architecture – a blend of carefully preserved older buildings and gleaming new skyscrapers – express a part of this split personality, while the working class, immigrant character of much of the city brushes up against the Boston Brahmin persona. This most historic of American cities is also continually revived by the flow of students to its many educational facilities, which adds fresh blood to the mix and ensures the city is forward-looking.

TWO CITIES IN ONE

The graceful Charles River splits Boston to the south from the separate city of Cambridge, home to the Ivy League institutions Harvard and MIT, to the north. For all practical purposes the two cities interact as one, and Boston's efficient, clean, and safe subway system (known simply as the 'T') makes shuttling between the two sides a breeze. Walkers and cyclists can also make use of dedicated paths traversing eight bridges between Harvard and the river's mouth into the harbor.

SEAT OF LEARNING

Spreading out from this central neighborhood is Greater Boston, which consists of nearly 100 towns with a total population of about 4.6 million. A not insignificant portion of that number is made up of young people who flock to the area's multiple seats of higher education, of which Harvard and MIT are the cream of the crop. Boston University alone – its campus dominating the area around Commonwealth Avenue west of Kenmore Square – has 30,000 students enrolled. All this adds up to a liberal and vibrant atmosphere for a city that respects its past, but also has one foot striding into the future.

ETHNIC DIVERSITY

The Boston area has long been a magnet for immigrants. The community most associated with the city are the Irish: those that claim Irish ancestry currently make up about 21.6 per cent of the population and remain the largest ethnic group, with a strong cultural influence in areas such as Jamaica Plain and South Boston. The Italian community, most visible in the North End, gave the city its former mayor, Thomas Menino – a popular politician and the first non-Irish mayor since 1884. After Menino left office, Boston returned to form electing Irish-Amer-

Dawn over Boston Harbor and the Financial District

ican Marty Walsh as its new mayor. Rounding out the city's ethnic diversity are more recent immigrants from Brazil, Vietnam, and China.

Boston Brahmins

For all this multiculturalism, Boston remains best-known for its Brahmins – the blue-blooded stock who can trace their ancestry back to the original 17th-century inhabitants of Massachusetts Bay Colony. Thanks to the philanthropic inclinations of many old Bostonian families, the city can share with one and all a treasure trove of art and culture, such as that on display at the wonderful Museum of Fine Arts. If this is what you are interested in, then a trip to nearby Salem to view the equally impressive collections of the Peabody Essex Museum is also recommended.

Boston lingo

Native Bostonians have a distinctive way of talking. The accent tends to result in an elongated 'a' and elided 'r' – hence 'Hahvahd Yahd', rather than Harvard Yard. Once you have got used to that, memorize the following commonly used shorthand to some of the city's locations: Com Ave – Commonwealth Avenue; JP – Jamaica Plain; Mass Ave – Massachusetts Avenue; Mem Drive – Memorial Drive; The Pike – The Massachusetts Turnpike.

ARCHITECTURAL DEVELOPMENT

What comes to mind when most people think of Boston's architecture are red-brick terrace houses and the golden dome of the State House. People used to the strict grid plan of other American cities are also wrong-footed by the meandering roads of its more historical areas, such as Downtown, the North End, and Charlestown. However, over the four centuries since it was settled, much has changed in Boston's built landscape, and, like any dynamic city, it is still evolving.

The Colonial era

Not much from the early Colonial period is left in Boston, mainly because

---

The end of the 'Big Dig'

The project to bury the Central Artery – the raised highway that sliced the harbor off from the Downtown area – in a tunnel beneath the city was known as the Big Dig. It took over a decade to complete, causing massive disruption, and cost in excess of $15 billion, making it one of the most expensive and controversial American civil engineering projects of recent times. The results, though, have widely been welcomed. Traffic flows much more freely across the city now, and the harbor and previously cut-off neighborhoods such as the North End are directly accessible via a pleasant strip of parkland known as the Rose F Kennedy Greenway. The highway emerges from its tunnel to cross the spectacular Leonard P. Zakim Bridge, named after a local civil-rights activist.

Old State House

the predominantly wooden houses of those days fell victim to frequent fires. Even as late as 1872 Boston was suffering catastrophic blazes: the Great Fire of that year wiped out most of the city center. The sole wooden construction from the 17th century that remains in central Boston is the Paul Revere House, built in 1680. The city burghers learned their lesson from

DON'T LEAVE BOSTON WITHOUT...

Seeing where American independence began. Pay homage to the original Tea Party participants at the Boston Tea Party Ships and Museum on the Waterfront, housed in replicas of the three ships that were involved in the momentous 1773 rebellion, later said by John Adams to be 'the spark that ignited the American Revolution.' See page 76.

Admiring art treasures in a Venetian-style palazzo. The Isabella Stewart Gardner Museum is a unique experience in Boston; artworks arranged in a distinctively personal style in a delightful palazzo, complete with peaceful gardens. See page 69.

Mingling with students at an Ivy League college. Cross the Charles River to Cambridge to visit prestigious Harvard or cutting-edge MIT and soak up the atmosphere of learning. See pages 42 and 50.

Finding the Underground Railroad. The Underground Railroad was a network of secret routes used by runaway black slaves before the American Civil War. To find out about this and Boston's 19th-century African-American community, visit the fascinating Museum of African American History in Beacon Hill. See page 55.

Tucking into Italian cuisine in the North End. Boston's Little Italy is a delightful neighborhood for wandering in, full of narrow lanes and hodgepodge buildings, with a proliferation of tempting places to eat. See page 35.

Swanning around. Ever since 1877, taking a turn on the Swan Boats (www.swanboats.com) on the lagoon of the Public Garden has been a fixture of the Boston scene. The paddle boats, which have been continuously operated by the Paget family, run from mid-April to mid-September, typically from 10am to 4pm. See page 57.

Seeing the home of the Red Sox. The city's baseball team are so popular that tickets for a game are snapped up as swiftly as they go on sale. Check the Red Sox website for what's available, or turn up early (real early) on match day for standing-room-only tickets, sold from the Gate C ticket window. Alternatively, take a tour of the hallowed pitch. See page 64.

Making an historic excursion. Travel out of town to explore great American literary heritage in Concord, a revolutionary road in Lexington, the landing site of the first pilgrims in Plymouth, or Salem, forever associated with witch-hunts. See page 87, page 90, and page 80.

these conflagrations and ditched wood in favor of brick and stone.

The 18th and 19th centuries
The architect most associated with Boston is Charles Bulfinch (1763–1844). The scion of a wealthy family, he traveled Europe soaking up ideas and influences that he later translated into the designs of friends' houses in Beacon Hill. The success of the homes led to Bulfinch being commissioned to design the new State House in 1798, which was something of a dry run for his US Capitol Building in Washington, DC.

By the early decades of the 19th century, land-reclamation projects were changing the shape of the city. Where the handsome terraces and garden squares of the South End and the grand mansions and boulevards of Back Bay now stand was once sea water and swamp. Boston's accumulated wealth and culture is reflected in the elaborate buildings from this era, such as the Ames-Webster Mansion, built in 1872, and the even more flamboyant Burrage House (1889).

Italian Renaissance, neo-Gothic, and neo-Romanesque styles were all the rage. You can spot all these motifs around Copley Square, which is crowned by the Boston Public Library, designed by Charles McKim (1847–1909) and one of the city's most impressive public buildings. Facing the library is Trinity Church, a masterpiece by Henry Hobson Richardson (1838–86), another great American architect.

The 20th century
Boston got its first skyscraper in 1915, but high-rise buildings never really caught on here. The Prudential Tower (1965) and John Hancock Tower (1975) stand out mainly because there are so few other skyscrapers in the city. Boston's style of contemporary inner-city regeneration has, instead, been on a more human scale. First came the demolition of the old West End and construction of Government Center – a not entirely harmonious project that is softened by the success of the nearby Faneuil Hall-Quincy Market complex. Rising real-estate prices helped revive Back Bay and later the South End, both of which fell into decline in the middle of the 20th century.

The 21st century
The completion of the massive engineering project known as the Big Dig has reconnected the city with the harbor, enabling the focus to shift to the South Boston Seaport district. Here you will find the Institute of Contemporary Art, which, along with the Frank Gehry-designed Stata Center over in the Massachusetts Institute of Technology (MIT), is a contemporary example of the cutting-edge architecture that Boston has dabbled in right through its history. The Foster + Partners' Art of the Americas Wing at the Museum of Fine Arts and Renzo Piano's addition to the Isabella Stewart Gardner Museum are lessons in how to harmoniously integrate new architecture with beloved classics.

Boston Public Library and New Old South Church

TOP TIPS FOR EXPLORING BOSTON

Half-price tickets. The Bostix booths beside Faneuil Hall (Tue–Sat 10am–6pm, Sun 11am–4pm) and on the corner of Copley Square (same hours; www.arts-boston.org) sell half-price tickets for many events (cash only) on performance day.

Live music. Check out the Weekly Dig (http://digboston.com) or Timeout Boston (www.timeout.com/boston) to see who and what is playing around town, and for the low-down on the hottest clubs.

Ticket saving. From April to November you can buy the Freedom Trail Ticket ($14, $8 for 3–12 years) which covers the Old South Meeting House, Paul Revere House, and the Old State House.

Visitor information. Boston's main Visitor Information Center (tel: 617-536-4100; www.bostonusa.com; daily 8.30am–5pm) is located on the northeastern edge of Boston Common, just south of the Park Street subway station (corner of Park and Tremont streets). You can pick up free maps and book tours here.

Free Shakespeare. A midsummer tradition is the Free Shakespeare on the Common, with performances held on Boston Common from mid-July to late August. See www.commshakes.org for details.

Library tours. There are often fine-art and photography exhibitions in the Boston Public Library. Free art and architecture tours depart from Dartmouth Street lobby in the old wing (Mon 2.30pm, Tue 6pm, Wed 11am, Thu 6pm, Fri and Sat 11am).

Duck Tours. Departing from Huntington Avenue, between Copley Place and the Prudential Center, are the popular Duck Tours (www.bostonducktours.com; mid-Mar–Nov 9am–dusk; $42), which use amphibious vehicles built in World War II (nicknamed 'ducks') for the 90-minute narrated land and water circuit around Boston. Advance booking is advised.

SoWa events. The first Friday of the month, between 5 and 9pm, members of the SoWa Artist Guild open up their studios. In May they also organize the weekend SoWa Art Walk (www.sowaboston.com).

Harbor islands camping. Four islands – Lovells, Grape, Peddocks and Bumpkin – allow camping from late June to early September for a small fee. Reservations can be made with the Department of Conservation and Recreation (toll free reservations: 1-877-422-6762, customer service: 1-877-620-2267) or by visiting the Boston Harbor Islands website (www.bostonharborislands.org/campground-reservations). Bring a picnic, as only Georges and Spectacle have snack bars in the summer season.

Whale watching. Cape Ann Whale Watch (www.seethewhales.com) runs whale-watching cruises from Rose Wharf, Gloucester. Online tourist information is available at www.seecapeann.com, www.capeannvacations.com, and www.rockportusa.com. For a whale-watching trip from Plymouth try Captain John Boats (www.captjohn.com).

Cape Cod lobster

FOOD AND DRINK

Once famous for its baked beans and meat-and-two-veg dinners, Boston cuisine today is equal parts traditional and contemporary. Beer is taken seriously, but there are also cool cocktail bars and hip cafés in which to relax.

LOCAL SPECIALTIES

New England cooking is all about traditional American produce, such as cranberries, corn, and seafood. Local specialties include creamy clam chowder, scrod (small, tender haddock or cod), steamers (clams with broth and butter), and lobster rolls.

Beer city

Founding father Samuel Adams was a brewmaster, which explains why Boston's principal brewery adopted his name. Having started out as a micro-brewery in 1985, Sam Adams (www.samueladams. com) now produces a fine range of ales found in bars across the city. Micro-breweries that have stayed truly micro include Boston Beer Works (www.beerworks.net), which has branches near Fenway Park and the North End, John Harvard's Brew House (www.johnharvards.com) near Harvard Square, and Cambridge Brewing Company (www.cambrew.com) near MIT. Bukowski Tavern (bukowskitavern.net) in Back Bay and Cambridge stocks over 100 different brews.

As you would expect for somewhere on the coast, you will find plenty of this style of cuisine in Boston itself.

Back in the 18th century Boston was awash with molasses shipped in from the Caribbean as part of the rum trade. These were mixed with salt pork and beans to make baked beans, once the quintessential Boston dish – hence the nickname Beantown. These days baked beans are not a common menu item; if you fancy trying them, Union Oyster House (see page 111) and Durgin Park (see page 117) both serve the dish.

HUMBLE TO HIGH-CLASS

Some of the city's best dining experiences are in the humblest of joints, be it enjoying a hearty breakfast or sandwich at Charlie's Sandwich Shoppe (see page 73) or simply delicious fish and chips at The Daily Catch (see page 41). That said, Boston also has a well-deserved reputation for contemporary American dining, as practiced by celebrity chefs such as Ken Oringer, of Uni and Toro (see pages 115 and 117), Todd English of Figs (see page 111), and Barbara Lynch of No. 9 Park (see page 114) and

A landmark restaurant   *Watermelon beer at Beer Works*

Sportello (see page 77).

ETHNIC AND TRENDY

Boston's diverse immigrant population has bequeathed it a fine range of ethnic restaurants.

Chinatown is primarily packed with Chinese restaurants, but it also has a smattering of Malaysian, Vietnamese, and Japanese eateries too.

The North End's vibe is almost exclusively Italian – from simple red-and-white-tablecloth cafés to sleek temples to regional *cucine*. For the trendiest dining spots, the South End and its SoWa (South of Washington) district are the places to head – between Tremont Street and Washington Avenue.

Seafood is a big feature of the Waterfront and up-and-coming Fort Point Channel areas, while the academic areas around Harvard and MIT are prime hunting grounds for good-value, atmospherically vibrant, and cosmopolitan restaurants and cafés. Cambridge's reputation for healthy organic cooking is deserved, but the town is also no slouch at fine dining. When it comes to discovering hot new chefs, it is this side of the Charles River that often proves the most fertile.

Reservations

Boston is not New York, so scoring a table at even the hottest places is well within reach. Nevertheless, you would be well advised to make an advance booking for Friday or Saturday nights: try the online booking service www.opentable.com. Note that some places do not take reservations at all, so turn up early or be prepared to wait.

BARS

The immigrant community most associated with Boston is that from Ireland. Therefore, Irish bars are prevalent in the city. A few are authentic, and worth visiting for a pint; others are tourist traps and best avoided.

Hip cocktail bars are also catching on, but Boston is too small a town to generate the kind of happening scene you would find in New York or London.

CAFÉS

It is hard to beat the North End's collection of cafés for an espresso or cappuccino, but gourmet coffee can also be had beside Boston Common at Thinking Cup (see page 33). Tea-lovers might enjoy Tealuxe (0 Brattle Street; www.tealuxe.com) in Harvard.

> ## Food and drink prices
>
> Price guide for a three-course dinner for one, excluding beverages, tax, and tip:
> $$$$ = above $60
> $$$ = $40–60
> $$ = $20–40
> $ = below $20

Faneuil Hall Marketplace

SHOPPING

Boston's shopping does not stop at Red Sox souvenirs. While tourists flock to the retail hubs of Faneuil Hall–Quincy Market and Newbury Street, do not miss the variety of shops that are tucked away.

BEACON HILL

Beacon Hill is known for tradition and history, so it is no surprise that over 40 antiques shops and art galleries have congregated here on Charles Street. The Sloane Merrill Gallery (no. 75; www.sloanemerrillgallery.com) specializes in showcasing living artists who paint oils using traditional techniques. Eugene Galleries at (no. 76; http://eugenegalleries.com) offers fine prints, etchings, and old maps, while E.R. Butler & Co. (no. 38; www.erbutler.com) carries distinctive hardware and tableware inspired by historical designs.

BACK BAY

The best range of shops is found around Back Bay. Newbury Street, often referred to as Boston's Rodeo Drive, offers the nicest retail experience and is renowned for its boutiques, art galleries, and quirky stores, particularly at the Massachusetts Avenue end. Riccardi (no. 116; www.riccardiboston.com) caters to the hip crowd, with fashions fresh off the runway. Root around The Closet (No. 175) has bargains on pre-loved high-end garments. John Fluevog (no. 302; www.fluevog.com) carries enough trendy shoes to satisfy even Imelda Marcos, while Johnny Cupcakes (no. 279; www.johnnycupcakes.com) is the place for kooky cool T-shirts and Shreve, Crump & Low (www.shrevecrumpandlow.com), Boston's answer to Tiffany's, has a home at 39 Newbury Street.

MALLS

Further along Boylston, the foot of the Prudential Tower is surrounded by the Prudential Center shopping mall (www.prudentialcenter.com). This is connected via an enclosed footbridge to another mall, ritzy Copley Place (www.simon.com), where you will find Barneys, selling up-and-coming designers, and the fancy department store Neiman Marcus. Across the Charles River, Cambridgeside Galleria (www.cambridgesidegalleria.com), on Route 4 or easily accessed from Lechmere T station, offers up around 120 brand-name stores in one location.

Cambridgeside Galleria   *Harvard Book Store*

THE SOUTH END

One shopping area often overlooked by visitors is the South End. It is dotted with interesting independent shops and is a haven for art-lovers and epicureans. The epicenter of Boston's commercial contemporary art scene is Harrison Avenue. Bobbie From Boston carries an impressive collection of vintage garments; designers from Ralph Lauren shop here for inspiration.

For modern design homewares, visit Lekker (www.lekkerhome.com), on the corner of Washington and Waltham streets, and Hudson (www.hudson-boston.com) at 12 Union Park Street. Tucked away in a courtyard at 46 Waltham Street is Patch NYC (www.patchnyc.com), another good place to find homewares as well as unique stocking gifts and decorative art. Around the block on Shawmut Avenue, Michele Mercaldo (no. 276; http://michelemercaldo.com) offers one-of-a-kind fine jewelry. South End Formaggio (no. 268; http://southendformaggio.com), arguably Boston's best deli, offers free wine-and-cheese tastings.

HARVARD SQUARE

Over in Cambridge, despite many chain stores moving in, Harvard Square still maintains an academic atmosphere with J. August (1320 Massachusetts Avenue); Harvard Bookstore (1256 Massachusetts Avenue; www.harvard.com), specializing in used and remainders; Grolier (6 Plympton Street; www.grolierpoetry-bookshop.org), offering America's largest poetry selection; Harvard Coop Bookstore (1400 Massachusetts Ave) and the children's bookstore Curious George Goes to Wordsworth (1 John F. Kennedy Street). Browsing the Museum of Useful Things on the corner of John F. Kennedy and Brattle streets is sure to turn up that useful something you never knew you needed.

DOWNTOWN AND FORT POINT

Downtown Crossing's shopping scene has expanded in recent years. Macy's has been joined by a variety of international chains, including Primark and TJ Maxx. Specialty stores such as Bromfield Camera (10 Bromfield Street; www.bromfieldcamera.com), which has been serving photographers since 1965, are also located here.

Unsurprisingly, tourists love Faneuil Hall-Quincy Market (www.faneuilhallmarketplace.com), with over 100 local and national name stores. Check out Boston Pewter Company (www.bostonpewtercompany.com) in the basement of Faneuil Hall, or the Revolutionary Boston Museum Shop in Quincy Market. Fort Point shopping took a major leap forward with the relocation of designer store Louis (www.louisboston.com) to Fan Pier. The arts and crafts of the many artists who work and live in the area can be found at Made in Fort Point (30 Channel Center Street). The shop at the ICA is also worth a look for art books, objets d'art, and jewelry.

Red Socks fans at Fenway Park

SPORT AND ENTERTAINMENT

Baseball and football dominate the sports seen in Boston, with a city–wide devotion to the Red Sox and the Patriots respectively. The student population also makes this a great place to party, with a range of musical and theatrical offerings every night.

BASEBALL

Sport runs in Boston's blood, none more so than the Red Sox (www.mlb.com/redsox). In 2004 the city's Major League Baseball team finally broke the losing 'curse' in the World Series championships that had haunted them for 86 years – ever since the legendary slugger Babe Ruth was sold to eternal rivals, the New York Yankees. To prove their new-found form, the Red Sox snatched another World Series victory in 2007, much to the delight of Bostonians, and then again in 2013 – an extra-special event, as this series win came at Fenway Park.

FOOTBALL, HOCKEY, AND BASKETBALL

The Red Sox can now stand proudly shoulder to shoulder with the city's American football team, the New England Patriots (www.patriots.com). One of the most successful teams in NFL history, the 'Pats' are five-time winners of the Super Bowl. Their home field is Gillette Stadium in Foxborough, 22 miles (35km) south of Boston, and the season runs from late August to late December.

From October to mid-April at the TD Garden stadium, you can catch the games of the city's ice hockey team, the Bruins (www.nhl.com/bruins), or the basketball team, the Celtics (www.nba.com/celtics). For all the hoopla over the Red Sox, it is the Celtics who are the most successful team in any major sport in the country. Beginning in 1959, they won an unprecedented eight National Basketball Association (NBA) championships on the trot, and to date have 17 NBA wins to their credit.

CLASSICAL MUSIC, OPERA, AND BALLET

Offering everything from garage-band rock to orchestral works, Boston is one of the US's most musically diverse cities. For classical music, check out the concert schedule of the beautiful Symphony Hall (301 Massachusetts Avenue; www.bso.org), which hosts the world-class Boston Symphony Orchestra, founded in 1881, from September to April; the orchestra can also be heard occasionally playing outdoors at the Hatch Shell in the Esplanade, where you may also catch the Symphony's spin-off Boston Pops Orchestra. Another excellent venue is Jordan Hall at

Boston Celtics at the TD Garden Stadium

the New England Conservatory of Music (30 Gainsborough Street; http://necmusic.edu), which stages many free concerts alongside ones by established ensembles, such as the Boston Philharmonic (www.bostonphil.org).

Opera, not Boston's strong point, is covered by the Boston Lyric Opera (www.blo.org) and the Boston Opera Collaborative (www.bostonoperacollaborative.org). However, the Boston Ballet (http://bostonballet.org) is considered one of the top dance companies in the US.

ROCK AND POP

The stars of rock and pop regularly turn up at the city's biggest venues, such as the outdoor Blue Hills Bank Pavilion (May–Sept only) out on South Boston Waterfront, and T.D. Garden (www.tdgarden.com), or medium-sized spaces such as House of Blues (15 Landsdowne Street; www.houseofblues.com) or the Orpheum Theater (1 Hamilton Place; http://crossroadspresents.com/orpheum-theatre). However, with all those students around, there is an enormous range of small live music venues and a thriving indie rock scene of bands and singers to fill them. Check out places such as the Brighton Music Hall and Paradise Rock Club (see page 120 for nightlife listings).

THEATER

Boston has a small but lively theater scene, with the city's grandest theaters, such as the Wang and the Shubert, often used for try-outs of Broadway-bound productions.

The most reliable places for interesting productions are The American Repertory Theatre (Loeb Drama Center, 64 Brattle Street; www.americanrepertorytheater.org) over in Harvard, the Huntington (www.huntingtontheatre.org), and the South End's Boston Center for the Arts (www.bcaonline.org), which has no fewer than four stages.

The Boston Marathon

Since 1897, Patriot's Day – the third Monday in April – has seen city traffic come to a standstill for the running of the Boston Marathon (www.baa.org), making this the world's oldest annually contested long-distance running race. That first 26-mile (42km) race began with just 15 participants, but today the marathon regularly has over 25,000 runners, including Olympic champions. The toughest section is the aptly named Heartbreak Hill, which rises up 80ft (24.3m) in the city's Newton Hills area. A half-marathon held in early October attracts up to 7,500 runners. Following the tragic events that occurred at 2013's Boston Marathon – when two pressure cooker bombs exploded, killing three people and injuring a further 264 – there was determination to make 2014's race the best ever; 36,000 people ran and over a million people came to watch the race.

Townsmen dressed as Indians dumping tea during the Boston Tea Party, 1773

HISTORY: KEY DATES

Settled by Native Americans for thousands of years before John Cabot claimed Massachusetts for King Henry VII of England in 1497, the Boston area is famous for its key role in American Independence.

PRE-REVOLUTIONARY BOSTON

1620	Pilgrims land at Plymouth Rock, just a few miles away from Boston.
1625	Colonist William Blackstone settles on the Common.
1630	Puritan English settlers led by John Winthrop form Massachusetts Bay Company colony at Charlestown.
1635	Boston Latin School, the nation's first public school, is founded.
1636	Harvard College is founded.
1684	Massachusetts Bay Company is made into a royal colony with a governor appointed by the king.
1692	The Salem Witch Trials begin.
1761	Boston lawyer James Otis declares: 'Taxation without representation is tyranny.'
1764	The Sugar Act and the Stamp Act arouse anti-royalist sentiments.

THE BATTLE FOR INDEPENDENCE

1770	Boston Massacre: British soldiers open fire killing 5 people.
1773	Boston Tea Party.
1775	Paul Revere's ride and battles of Lexington and Concord spark the American Revolution. Battle of Bunker Hill and burning of Charlestown. George Washington takes command of army at Cambridge.
1776	British troops withdraw from Massachusetts. Declaration of Independence is announced from the Old State House on July 18th.
1789	US Constitution is framed; John Hancock is declared first governor of the state of Massachusetts.

19TH CENTURY

1812	War of 1812 against the British paralyzes the city's commerce.

Robert Gould Shaw and the 54th Regiment Memorial (see Route 5)

1822	Boston is finally incorporated as a city on March 4th
1841	First Irish immigrants arrive.
1857	Filling of Back Bay begins.
1861–5	American Civil War.
1872	Great Fire of Boston.
1881	Frederick Law Olmsted begins work on Emerald Necklace parks.
1897	First Boston Marathon. America's first subway opens at Park Street.

20TH CENTURY

1903	Boston is the site of first World Series – the Red Sox win.
1919	Strike of 1,300 Boston police. Breaking it brings to national prominence Massachusetts Governor Calvin Coolidge.
1920	The Red Sox sell Babe Ruth to the New York Yankees.
1946	John Fitzgerald Kennedy is elected Congressman for Charlestown and Cambridge.
1980s	The 'Massachusetts Miracle' high-tech revolution results in an economic boom.
1990	Thieves remove $200 million in paintings from Isabella Stewart Gardner Museum in the largest art heist in history.

21ST CENTURY

2001	Two planes departing from Boston Logan International Airport are hijacked and crash into the World Trade Center in NYC.
2004	The Red Sox break 86-year losing streak by winning the World Series. The US's first legally recognized same-sex wedding takes place. Harvard students set up social networking site Facebook.
2008	Boston Celtics win the NBA championships for the 17th time.
2009	Thomas Menino becomes Boston's longest serving mayor.
2013	Two bombs explode at the finish line of the Boston Marathon, killing three and injuring many others.
2014	Marty Walsh elected as mayor of Boston.
2016	Massachusetts residents vote to legalize marijuana.
2017	The New England Patriots stage the biggest comeback in Super Bowl history, winning the Super Bowl in overtime 34-28.
2018	Desiree Linden becomes the first American female to win the Boston Marathon in 33 years.

BEST ROUTES

Shady spot on Boston Common

BOSTON COMMON AND DOWNTOWN

Covering the first half of the historic Freedom Trail, this route runs from Boston Common, the city's geographical and social crossroads, through Downtown, to the oldest continuously run restaurant in the US.

DISTANCE: 1.5 miles (2.5km)
TIME: A half day
START: Boylston T Station
END: Haymarket T Station
POINTS TO NOTE: Downtown is busy with office workers Monday to Friday, particularly around lunchtime, so a good time to do this walk is early morning after rush hour or at the weekend. On Friday and Saturday there is also a lively fresh-produce market at Haymarket. If you do the walk in the afternoon, you could finish with dinner in Chinatown and a show in the Theater District.

Starting at Boston Common, one of the oldest sections of the city, and ending at the cobblestone streets of Blackstone Block, this walk will take you deep into Boston's history. During its 360-plus years the Common has been a popular spot for sermons, promenades, and, in the years before the Revolution, political protest. Stroll through it today and you will see everyone from Chinese women practicing tai chi in the shade of ancient elm trees to rappers and break-dancers showing off their skills, and office workers from Downtown's modern skyscrapers grabbing some fresh air while enjoying their lunch.

The Freedom Trail

Most of this route follows a section of the 2.5-mile (4km) Freedom Trail. This runs through the heart of Boston past 16 significant sites that are among the city's oldest landmarks and featured in the decisive break that New England's settlers made from the British in 1776. Established in 1958 to preserve these key monuments and sites, the Trail is marked by a red-brick or painted line on the pavement. It is relatively easy to follow, but if you would prefer, **The Freedom Trail Foundation** (www.thefreedomtrail. org) offers daily guided tours from the Visitor Information Center or Faneuil Hall.

BOSTON COMMON

This walking route starts at the southeast corner of **Boston Common**, at the junction of Boylston and Tremont streets.

Cutler Majestic Theatre   *Freedom Trail sidewalk sign*

The Common, established in 1634, is the oldest public park in the US and a storybook of Boston history. Originally used as a 'Comon Field' *(sic)* on which sheep and cattle grazed (they did so up until 1830), the pentagonal space, covering about 50 acres (20 hectares), was also used as a mustering ground for militias and a venue for public hangings. Among those who met a cruel end dangling from the Great Elm, which stood on the Common until 1876, was Mary Dyer, the heroic Quaker who insisted on the right to worship freely. A statue in her memory stands outside the State House on the corner of Beacon and Bowdon streets.

Central Burying Ground
Immediately to the left as you face the Common from the corner of Boylston Street is the **Central Burying Ground ❶** (daily dawn–dusk). During the American Revolution the Common was transformed into a British military center. As many as 2,000 Redcoats were quartered here during Boston's occupation, and several dozen British soldiers killed at the Battle of Bunker Hill were interred in the cemetery. It is the city's fourth-oldest cemetery, but few of note are buried here. One exception is Gilbert Stuart (1755–1828) who painted the classic portrait of George Washington.

Soldiers and Sailors Monument
The western part of the Common is devoted to athletic endeavor, with a well-patronized baseball field and tennis courts. Head north from the burying ground, watching out for scampering grey squirrels, past the pretty Parkman Bandstand, to admire the 70ft (21m) **Soldiers and Sailors Monument ❷**, located atop Telegraph Hill. It is dedicated to the Union forces killed in the Civil War.

Frog Pond
Close by is **Frog Pond ❸**, used as a children's wading pool in summer and an ice rink in winter. In Colonial times sheep and cows slaked their thirst at this watering hole. Later, Bostonians fished in it for minnows in the summer and ice-skated on it in the winter, and here they celebrated the first arrival of piped-in municipal water from a suburban reservoir in 1848. Sadly, lined with concrete today, the pond is no longer a home for minnows nor frogs.

PARK STREET

Exit the Common at its northeast corner on Park Street. If you fancy refreshments at this point, you can backtrack down Tremont Street to find **Thinking Cup**, see ①.

Just north of Park Street T Station, on the corner of Park and Tremont streets, stands **Park Street Church ❹** (www. parkstreet.org; mid-June–Aug Tue–Sat 9.30am–3pm), with its majestic 217ft (66m) steeple (adapted from a Christopher Wren design). William Lloyd Garrison delivered his first anti-slavery speech here in 1829.

Parkman Bandstand, Boston Common

OLD GRANARY BURYING GROUND

Next to the church, on Tremont Street, pay your respects at the grave of Paul Revere, Samuel Adams, John Hancock, and other key revolutionary figures in the illustrious **Old Granary Burying Ground** ❺ (9am–5pm, winter until 3pm), dating from 1660. The graveyard is named after the granary that was demolished to make way for the Park Street Church. Opposite is Bosworth St at the end of which is the sandwich shop **Sam La Grassa's**, see ❷.

OMNI PARKER HOUSE HOTEL

Return to Tremont Street and continue to the corner with School Street, past the fancy Venetian facade of the Tremont Temple Baptist Church (once a famous Boston theater), where stands the **Omni Parker House Hotel** ❻, the oldest continuously operating hotel in the US. The present building is not the original, but much of the lobby's ornately carved wooden decoration is. Pop inside to see where Charles Dickens conducted literary seminars, the Vietnamese leader Ho Chi Minh waited on tables, and Malcolm X toiled in the kitchen. The hotel lays claim to inventing a couple of Boston's culinary favourites – Boston cream pie and the Parker Roll, a soft bread roll.

KING'S CHAPEL AND BURYING GROUND

On the corner of School and Tremont streets is **King's Chapel** ❼ (www.kingschapel.org; Mon–Sat 10am–5pm Sun 1.30–5pm, winter until 4pm, services Wed 6pm and Sun 11am). The present granite structure dates from 1754, but the chapel had its origins in the 1680s, when Britain's King James II made a colossal political blunder by sending

Around Chinatown

Close to the route's start, immediately east of Bolyston Street, are Boston's Chinatown and Theater District, areas you will likely want to return to for dining and evening entertainment. At the intersection of Surface Road and Beach Street (Chinatown's main drag) is an ornate *paifang*, a traditional-style Chinese gateway flanked by a pair of stone foo lions. The area around it has recently been landscaped into an attractive garden with bamboo and water features – a result of Downtown beautification after the Big Dig (see page 12). Chinatown might not be large, but it is packed with lively Asian restaurants and exotic stores. It is great fun to visit, and can easily be combined with a night out at one of the theaters on Stuart or Tremont streets, such as the Wang and Shubert, where for decades Broadway-bound productions have had their trial runs.

Omni Parker House Hotel   *King's Chapel*

to Boston a clergyman whose job was to install in the town the very thing the Puritans had hated and fled: a branch of the Church of England.

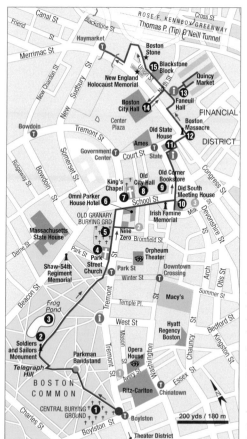

Next to the Chapel, on Tremont Street, is Boston's first cemetery, **King's Chapel Burying Ground** (daily 9am–5pm, winter until 3pm), in use from 1630 to 1796, thus predating the Anglican edifice whose name it later assumed. The Bay Colony's first governor, John Winthrop, was buried here in 1649.

The monument at the corner of the burying ground honors a French naval adjutant, the Chevalier de Saint-Sauveur, killed by a Boston mob in September 1778 during an altercation over bread. The French, who had come to help the colonials, were baking bread using their own stores of wheat; Bostonians, who were enduring a severe shortage of flour, were incensed when told that they could not buy the French Navy's bread. The Chevalier's funeral service is said to have been the first Catholic Mass in Boston.

OLD CITY HALL

Further down School Street is **Old City Hall** ❽

King's Chapel Burying Ground

(www.oldcityhall.com), built in 1865 in the French Second Empire style. When the city government decamped from here in 1969 for the new City Hall, this handsome edifice was preserved as a mixed-use complex of offices and a steak restaurant.

In the forecourt are bronze statues of Benjamin Franklin and Josiah Quincy, in his time a senator, Boston mayor, and president of Harvard. Pop into the hall's vestibule to read about the building's history and that of the Boston Latin School, the nation's first school, which once stood close to this spot – hence the name School Street. Look down the sidewalk outside and you will see a pretty hopscotch mosaic celebrating the school.

OLD CORNER BOOKSTORE

Continue to the intersection of School and Washington streets, where you will find the **Old Corner Bookstore** ❾, dating from 1712, and currently the Chipotle Mexican Grill. Over the years the building has served as an apothecary, a dry-goods store, and private residence, although it is fondly remembered in its 1828 incarnation as the home of the eminent Ticknor and Fields publishing firm and a bookstore. In the 'golden age' of American literature the store was a popular meeting place for Whittier, Emerson, Stowe, Alcott, and other distinguished writers.

In the small square opposite stands the **Irish Famine Memorial**, which honors the 37,000 Irish who emigrated to America in the mid-19th century in the wake of Ireland's potato famine.

OLD SOUTH MEETING HOUSE

Immediately to the right on Washington Street is the **Old South Meeting House** ❿ (www.oldsouthmeetinghouse. org; daily Apr–Oct 9.30am–5pm, Nov–Mar 10am–4pm), built in 1727 and styled after the graceful London chapels of Sir Christopher Wren. The church was the scene of the events that preceded the infamous Boston Tea Party of 1773 and the baptism on a chilly January 6, 1706, of Benjamin Franklin, born around the corner on Milk Street, where you will find the **Milk Street Café**, see ❸.

It was on December 16, 1773, at the Old South Meeting House, that more than 5,000 Bostonians met to decide what to do with three tea-laden ships in the harbor. Disguised as Mohawk Indians, a gang of colonists, enraged at the British tax placed on tea and other imports, ran down Milk Street to Griffins Wharf. The crowd followed, and, with cries of 'Boston harbor a teapot tonight!', 340 crates of tea were dumped overboard.

OLD STATE HOUSE

From the Old South Meeting House, continue north along Washington

Guide in Colonial dress

Clock atop the Old State House

Street toward the junction with State Street. Immediately to the right, overshadowed by modern skyscrapers, is the **Old State House** ⑪ (www.bostonhistory.org; daily 9am–5pm, June–early September until 6pm), Boston's oldest public building, built in 1713 as the seat of the Colonial government. It now houses a small museum. In 1787 John Hancock was inaugurated here as the first governor of the state under its new Constitution. You can recognize the building by those symbols of British imperial power, the lion and unicorn, the originals of which were thrown into the street when the Declaration of Independence was read from the balcony on July 18, 1776. On display inside are items relating to Boston's role in the Revolutionary War and other parts of the city's history.

BOSTON MASSACRE

Continuing along the Freedom Trail from the Old State House, it is easy to miss the circle of cobblestones on a tiny traffic island at the junction of State and Congress streets. This marks the spot of the **Boston Massacre** ⑫ where, on March 5, 1770, a handful of British soldiers fired into a jeering crowd that was pelting them with snowballs; five men were killed, including former slave Crispus Attucks, who is buried in the Old Granary Burying Ground.

FANEUIL HALL

Head north on Congress Street and turn right to reach **Faneuil Hall** ⑬ (www.faneuilhall.com). A statue of Samuel Adams, one of the Founding Fathers of the United States, stands in front this historic public hall, named after benefactor Peter Faneuil. Designated by patriot orator James Otis as the 'Cradle of Liberty,' it was here that the Sons of Liberty called many meetings of complaint about British taxation without representation.

The original hall was built in 1742; the current one was designed by Charles Bulfinch in 1805. Recent renovations have seen the **Boston National Historical Park Visitor Center** (www.nps.gov/bost; daily 9am–5pm) installed on the first floor along with various shops. Come here for information and for Ranger-led free daily walking tours along part of the Freedom Trail; see the website for details. Upstairs, if a public meeting is not taking place, a ranger also conducts a history talk every half hour in the Great Hall (daily 9am–4.30pm).

In the adjacent Quincy Market complex, which is covered in Route 10 (see page 74), you will find several places to eat.

BOSTON CITY HALL

On the western side of Congress Street, climb the concrete steps leading up to **Boston City Hall** ⑭. Prior to the con-

Irish Famine Memorial

struction in 1969 of this charmless inverted ziggurat, the area was known as Scollay Square, a slightly disreputable entertainment area. In the 1960s the Boston Redevelopment Authority decided to raze Scollay Square and the nearby tenements of the West End. The area was renamed Government Center, its focus the vast, empty, and depressing City Hall Plaza. Throughout the year various pop ups occur including an ice rink and beer festivals.

NEW ENGLAND HOLOCAUST MEMORIAL

Also far from uplifting, but beautiful in a melancholy way, are the six tall, slender glass-and-steel towers of the **New England Holocaust Memorial** in Carmen Park, a strip of greenery opposite the City Hall between Union and Congress streets. Forming a mute tribute to the those murdered by the Nazis in World War II, each glass column, wreathed in steam symbolizing the gas chambers, represents a different concentration camp and is inscribed with numbers – 6 million in total.

At the Faneuil Hall end of the park are two bronze statues of James Curley, the Irish politician who dominated Boston politics from 1920 to 1950, even managing to be re-elected while in jail.

BLACKSTONE BLOCK

In stark contrast to the concrete wastelands of Government Center are the charming brick buildings and cobbled lanes of **Blackstone Block** ⑮, which dates back to the 17th century and is named after Boston's first colonist, William Blackstone (who settled in the Boston Common area in 1625). The block is bounded by Union, Hanover, Blackstone, and North streets. At 41 Union Street is the historic **Union Oyster House** (see page 111), Boston's oldest brick house. A rare example of Georgian architecture in the city, the restaurant dates from at least 1660, when it was owned by Boston's first town crier, William Courser. Mentioned in a city plan of 1708, the

Taking a trolley

Several sightseeing 'trolleys' (in fact, conventional wheeled vehicles with trolley-like bodywork) run at roughly 15-minute intervals on routes around Boston's main sights. It is a great way to see the city, especially if time is limited. You can hop off wherever you like, explore on foot, and then board a later trolley – just make sure the trolley company matches your ticket. Operators include Old Town Trolley Tours (tel: 888-910-8687; www.trolleytours.com/Boston), City View Trolley Tours (tel: 617-363-7899; www.cityviewtrolleys.com), and Brush Hill Tours (tel: 800-343-1328; www.brushhilltours.com).

The Holocaust Memorial

The stark City Hall

house was the office of the *Massachusetts Spy* newspaper from 1771 to 1775, while in 1796 the exiled Louis-Philippe, who later became king of France, taught French in the rooms above James Amblard's tailor shop.

A few yards down Marshall Street (just off Union Street), opposite the 18th-century Ebenezer Hancock House at no. 10, look down to see the **Boston Stone**, a stone ball and stone trough built into the wall of a gift shop. Shipped from England in 1700 to serve as a paint mill, the stones were later used as the point from which all distances from Boston were measured. Their role as the hub of 'The Hub' was later taken over by the dome of the Massachusetts State House.

If it is Friday or Saturday, you might want to linger around here to enjoy the **fresh produce market** that wraps its way around North and Blackstone streets.

Otherwise, return to Congress Street, at the head of which is **Haymarket Station**, where you can finish this tour, or catch the T back to Boylston or Chinatown stations for dinner and a night at the theater. Alternatively, continue across the Rose F. Kennedy Greenway into the North End for the second half of the Freedom Trail.

Food and drink

① THINKING CUP

165 Tremont Street; tel: 617-482-5555; www.thinkingcup.com; Mon–Wed 7am–10pm, Thu–Sun 7am–11pm; $

Trade up from Starbucks at this sophisticated self-serve café serving much-praised Sumptown Coffee – they use only the finest beans from around the world. Add in a pastry, baked goodie, or sandwich and you're good to go.

② SAM LA GRASSA'S

44 Providence Street; tel: 617-357-6861; www.samlagrassas.com; Mon–Fri 11am–3.30pm; $

The sliced meats and cheeses are piled high on the many creative sandwiches available at this very popular Downtown café; signature sarnies include the Famouse Rumanian Pastrami and Pulled BBQ chicken. Salads and other treats are also available and you can eat in or take away.

③ MILK STREET CAFÉ

50 Milk Street; tel: 617-542-3663; www.milkstreetcafe.com; Mon–Fri 7am–3pm; $

Reasonable prices for generous portions is the deal at this kosher cafeteria, with dairy and fish, no meats. Find made-from-scratch dishes, such as roasted salmon salad and vegetable lasagne, and nutritious homemade soups.

St Stephen's Church and the Old North Church

THE NORTH END AND CHARLESTOWN

The second half of the Freedom Trail traverses the North End and Charlestown, two of Boston's oldest areas, packed with historical sites. The North End, Boston's Little Italy, is an especially pleasant place to return to in the evening for a meal.

DISTANCE: 2.5 miles (4.5km)
TIME: A half day
START: Haymarket T Station
END: Community College T Station
POINTS TO NOTE: This route follows on from the end of Route 1, and the two can be linked for a full day's itinerary. An alternative way to access or leave this route is by hopping on the Inner Harbor Ferry, which connects Charlestown Navy Yard with Long Wharf beside the Aquarium. Ferries run daily, every 15 minutes Mon–Fri between 6.30am and 8pm, every 30 minutes Sat–Sun between 10am and 6pm, and cost $3.50.

Much of the North End's charm as a neighborhood comes from its improvisational quality, with a hodgepodge of buildings – some quite attractive, others not, and many dating from the late 1800s, when they were used as tenement houses for European immigrants.

Hanover Street is the area's main thoroughfare, but around it spreads an archaic and somewhat confusing street plan. The North End is one of those places where it is easy to get lost, and probably best that you do. All kinds of unconventional spaces, not to mention many delicious delis, cafés, and restaurants can be discovered in the neighborhood's less traveled areas.

ROSE F KENNEDY GREENWAY

Begin the walk at **Haymarket T Station**. Until only a few years ago the raised expanse of the Fitzgerald Expressway (also known as the Central Artery) cut the North End off from the rest of the city. Now that the 'Big Dig' has buried the road underground, the cleared land forms a ribbon of parks through the city, known collectively as the **Rose F Kennedy Greenway** (www.rosekennedygreenway.org). Rose Fitzgerald Kennedy, mother of President John F. Kennedy, was born in the North End in 1890,

Paul Revere House   *Italian fare abounds in the North End*

and her funeral was conducted at St Stephen's Church on Hanover Street in 1995.

HANOVER STREET

Head southeast through the park until you reach Hanover Street. On either side, as the street cuts through the park, are railings inscribed with historical dates and quotations about the area from past residents.

As Hanover Street enters the North End it is almost wall-to-wall with cafés and restaurants. For an espresso to power your way stop at **Caffé Paradiso**, see ①. A bit further along the street, you will come to **Caffé Vittoria**, see ②, and **The Daily Catch**, see ③, which are both also recommended.

PAUL REVERE HOUSE

Turn right on Richmond Street and then left to enter cobbled North Square, where at no. 19 you will find the **Paul Revere House** ① (www.paulreverehouse. org; daily mid-Apr–Oct 9.30am–5.15pm, Nov–mid-Apr 9.30am–4.15pm, Jan–Mar, closed Mon).

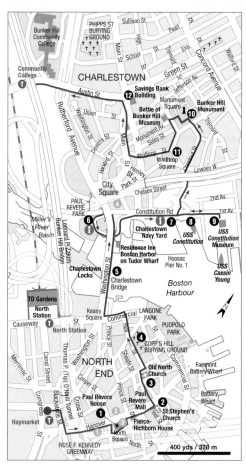

Inside Boston's oldest church

Built in 1680, this two-story dwelling, with an overhanging second floor, is downtown Boston's oldest wooden house. Revere, then a silversmith, took up residence in 1770, and the house is furnished today much as it was when it was home to him and the first Mrs Revere, who bore him eight children, and then, when she died, to the second Mrs Revere, who produced a similar brood. It is from here that Revere started his historic horse ride that warned, 'the British are coming!'

Pierce-Hichborn House

Next door is the restored **Pierce-Hichborn House** (open for guided tours only once or twice daily; see Paul Revere House website for details), which belonged to Nathaniel Hichborn, Revere's cousin. The asymmetrical, three-story brick building, built between 1711 and 1715 in the new English Renaissance style, was a radical departure from the Tudor-style wooden dwellings built in the previous century.

ST STEPHEN'S CHURCH

Exit North Square via Prince Street, following the red bricks of the Freedom Trail back to Hanover Street. Turn right and walk two blocks north to reach **St Stephen's Church ❷**, with its white steeple. Built in 1804 as a Congregationalist Meeting House, this dignified structure is the only one of five Boston churches designed by Charles Bulfinch

that still stands. In 1813 it became a Unitarian church, and in 1862 it was acquired by the Roman Catholic archbishopric. Eight years later, when Hanover Street had to be widened to accommodate traffic, the church was moved back 12ft (3.7m) and raised 6ft (1.8m); then, in 1965, it was restored to its original level.

PAUL REVERE MALL

Directly opposite St Stephen's Church is the **Paul Revere Mall**, known locally as the Prado. Built in 1933, this spacious brick courtyard is one of the liveliest public spaces in the North End – a sort of Americanized piazza where kids run around, old folks play cards, and footsore tourists take a breather from the Freedom Trail. In addition to a traditional Italian fountain, the Prado features a magnificent equestrian statue of Paul Revere, modeled in 1885 by Cyrus Dallin and cast in 1940. On the southern (left) wall, bronze panels recall the history of Boston and its people.

OLD NORTH CHURCH

At the far end of the Prado a small gate opens to the rear of Christ Church, more popularly known as **Old North Church ❸** (www.oldnorth.com; daily mid-Nov–Mar 10am–4pm, April–mid-Nov 9am–6pm). Before going into the church, take note on the left

Old North Church

of the three-story (originally it was two) brick home of Ebenezer Clough, built in 1712. Next to it is a small garden planted as it would have been in the 18th century, while opposite is a poignant reminder of a more modern event: a Memorial Garden hung with military dog tags for those who have perished in recent wars in Afghanistan and Iraq.

Built in 1723, Old North is Boston's oldest church. Its interior, painted white since 1912, sports high pew boxes, designed to keep in the warmth of braziers filled with hot coal or bricks, which were placed on the floor on wintry days. The clock at the rear of the church and the four baroque Belgian cherubs that surround it date back to the opening of the church. So does the organ case, although the actual instrument dates only from 1759. It is still played at the service every Sunday at 11am.

The bust of George Washington, in a niche to the left of the apse, was the first public memorial to the great man, and was said by General Lafayette in 1824 to be 'more like him than any other portrait.' The church has 37 crypts, containing, it is claimed, 1,100 bodies.

COPP'S HILL BURYING GROUND

Exit from the church, and walk northwest up Hull Street for about 150yds/m to **Copp's Hill Burying Ground** ❹ (daily dawn–dusk), Boston's second-oldest

North End history

On Colonial maps the North End looks like an irregular thumb jutting into the Atlantic Ocean, with a canal, called the Mill Stream, cutting it off from the larger Shawmut Peninsula.

By the late Colonial period the small cluster of wooden houses had become one of Boston's most fashionable quarters, with several fine brick homes and some of the richest families in town. Unfortunately, many of the prominent residents were Tories who, when the British evacuated in 1776, hightailed it to Canada and took their money with them. Rich Yankees pulled out too, preferring the more genteel atmosphere of Beacon Hill, then being developed. Artisans, sailors, and tradesmen filled the empty houses, and throughout the 19th century the North End was a working man's quarter dominated by the shipping industry.

The Irish poured into the neighborhood in the 1840s, and soon dominated the area politically. Eastern European Jews followed the Irish, and by 1890 had established a thriving residential and business district along Salem Street. The Italians – mostly from Sicily and the southern provinces of the mainland – were the last group to arrive in substantial numbers; by the 1920s they had established an overwhelming majority, and have dominated the neighborhood ever since.

Copp's Hill gravestones

cemetery (after King's Chapel), where the gravestones, some ornately carved, poke out of the grass like misshapen teeth. Its name comes from that of William Copp, who farmed on the hill's southeast slope in the mid-17th century. In the Colonial era, the base of the hill, known pejoratively as New Guinea (after the African country of Guinea), was occupied by the city's first black community, and about 1,000 black citizens are buried in the cemetery's northwest corner.

Opposite the main entrance to Copp's Hill Burying Ground, take note of the gray-painted clapboard house at 44 Hull Street. At just 9.5ft (3m) wide, this is Boston's narrowest home, allegedly built around 1800 by a spiteful man to block the light coming into the neighboring house.

Notable tombstones

In the graveyard's northeast corner a tall black monument commemorates Prince Hall, who helped found Boston's first school for black children, and who was also the founder, in 1784, of the African Grand Lodge of Massachusetts, the world's first black Masonic Lodge. Nearby is the tombstone of 'Capt. Daniel Malcolm, Mercht,' who is remembered for smuggling 60 casks of wine into port without paying the duty. He asked to be buried 'in a Stone Grave 10 feet deep,' secure from desecration. His body may have been safe, but his tombstone was not: on it are scars made by the Redcoats who singled it out for target practice.

CHARLESTOWN

The Freedom Trail's red-brick route leads you along Hull Street to Commercial Street, where you turn left and then right to cross the Charles River on the **Charlestown Bridge ❺**.

Ahead lies the city's oldest settlement, established in 1628, two years ahead of Boston. In 1630 it was the seat of the British government, and on its Breed's Hill the bloody Battle of Bunker Hill was fought on June 17, 1775. The area's prosperity was later tied up with the Navy Yard founded in 1800. At times (usually wartimes), it was the busiest shipbuilding and repair yard in the US, but in 1974 demand slowed to the point where the facility was forced to close – a third of it was taken over by the National Park Service.

Crossing the bridge provides an excellent view on the left of the **Charlestown Locks**, which control the water level between the river and the Inner Harbor, and, rising majestically in the background, the **Leonard P. Zakim Bunker Hill Bridge** (www.leonardp zakimbunkerhillbridge.org), one of the most striking contemporary structures in the city.

Paul Revere Park

Below the bridge on the Charlestown side of the river is pretty little **Paul**

Clapboard houses in the Bunker Hill neighborhood

Revere Park ❻, part of the Harbor-Walk. Take the steps down to the park and follow the walkway under the Charlestown Bridge and past the hotel on Tudor Wharf toward the Charlestown Navy Yard.

City Square

Before exploring the Charlestown Navy Yard, you could take a breather at **Sorelle Bakery and Café**, see ❹, facing onto **City Square**, to the north-west. In the square's center a small circle of greenery preserves the foundations of the Great House, dating from 1629 and believed to have been John Winthrop's home and the colony's brief seat of government. The house became the Three Cranes Tavern in 1635, and was destroyed during the Battle of Bunker Hill.

CHARLESTOWN NAVY YARD

Walk for 100yds/m or so along Constitution Road toward the entrance of **Charlestown Navy Yard** ❼, whose most famous resident is the USS *Constitution*. Just inside the entrance is the **Visitor Center** (www.nps.gov/bost; daily Sept–June 9am–5pm, July–Aug 9am–6pm), where you can find out about free tours of the ship and its neighbor, the restored naval destroyer USS *Cassin Young*, which served in the Pacific during World War II. Elsewhere in the National Park Service administered area you can wander around the old buildings and dry docks used to mend ships. Escape the crowds at the little-visited **Massachusetts Korean War Veterans Memorial**, where you can listen to recordings of veterans remembering the conflict.

USS Constitution

Boston-built and first sailed from here in 1797, the **USS *Constitution*** ❽ (www.nps.gov; daily 10am–6pm; tours every half-hour) is the world's oldest warship still in commission. It keeps this status thanks to an annual July 4 'turnaround,' when tugs pull it out into the harbor. During its active service between 1797 and 1855, the USS *Constitution* was a victor in 42 battles.

On board, Navy enlistees in 1812 uniform conduct guided tours and answer questions. During the busy summer months lines to tour the USS *Constitution* can be long.

Opposite the ship is the **USS *Constitution* Museum** ❾ (www.ussconstitutionmuseum.org; daily 9am–6pm), which simulates the experience of life below decks. You can place your hands on a ship's wheel, climb into a hammock, or hoist the sail on a moving 'deck' while the sounds of shipboard life echo all around. Also on show in the museum is a walk-through model of a keel and ribbing, and a continuous audiovisual program that depicts a bloody sea battle of 1812.

The USS Constitution

BUNKER HILL MONUMENT AND MUSEUM

Exit the Navy Yard back onto Constitution Road and turn right to reach Chelsea Street. Duck through the nearby underpass beneath the Tobin Bridge, emerging on Lowney Way. Turn left and then immediately right onto Chestnut Street. Continue along Chestnut Street to the **Bunker Hill Monument** ❿ (www.nps.gov; daily 9am–4.30pm, July–Aug until 5.30pm), a 220ft (67m) -high granite obelisk crowning Breed's Hill. The battle was fought just north of the monument.

Climb the 294 stairs to the top for rewarding views of the city. The bronze statue on a pedestal in front of the monument is Colonel William Prescott, the patriot who uttered the immortal line, 'Don't fire until you see the whites of their eyes!' as an instruction to the troops before the battle.

On the corner of Monument Square and Monument Avenue is the small **Battle of Bunker Hill Museum** (www. nps.gov; daily 9am–5pm), where, on the second floor, hangs an excellent reproduction of the *Bunker Hill Cyclorama*, a circular painting that places the viewer at the heart of the battle's action. The original was shown in 1888 at the now demolished Castle Square Theater at 421 Tremont Street in the South End.

WINTHROP SQUARE

From the southeast corner of Monument Square head downhill along Winthrop Street, which leads into picturesque **Winthrop Square** ⓫. For a century this was a training field where Charlestown boys learned the art of war. At the northwest corner is a gate flanked by bronze tablets commemorating those killed on June 17, 1775.

Weekend processions

If you are in Boston in summer, be sure to time your visit to the North End to catch one of the Italian community's local feasts, or *festas*, celebrated in honor of saints' days. They are held almost every weekend in July and August, with Sunday being by far the more exciting day, and usually involve street fairs, brass bands, singers, raffles, food stalls selling sausage and peppers and *zeppole* (fried dough), and processions in which saints' statues are carried, often festooned with contributions of paper money. In the Feast of the Madonna del Soccorso (Our Lady of Succor), celebrated in mid-August, the star of the show is the famous flying angel. Portrayed by a little girl on a pulley, she floats above North Street, her arms outstretched to the crowd, and is lowered to the statue and the procession below. The biggest celebrations are the Fisherman's Feast and St Anthony's Feast in late August.

Colonel Prescott statue and Bunker Hill Monument

Return to Winthrop Street and keep going downhill, past the fire station and across Warren Street until you reach the junction with Main Street. Turn right here and head a couple of blocks to the corner of Pleasant Street, where you'll find the historic **Warren Tavern** (see page 112) dating from 1780. Both Paul Revere and George Washington once stayed here.

SAVINGS BANK BUILDING

A few yards north, where Main Street meets Austin Street, stands the handsome Victorian Gothic-style **Savings Bank Building** ⑫ at 1 Thompson Square, built in 1875. The interior has been sensitively adapted into offices, a florist, barber, and café, with the bank's enormous vaults still left intact.

From here a short walk west along Austin Street and across busy Rutherford Avenue will bring you to **Community College Station**, behind Bunker Hill Community College, the end of this route.

Alternatively, amble back through Charlestown, admiring its many old homes, toward the Navy Yard to pick up the Inner Harbor Ferry to Long Wharf.

Food and drink

① CAFFÉ PARADISO
255 Hanover Street; tel: 617-742-1768; www.caffeparadisoboston.com; daily 7am–2am; $$
A popular local hangout, this café's espresso, cannoli, panini, and calzoni are particularly delicious. Sweets are displayed in a glass counter and the TV beams in soccer games from Italy via satellite.

② CAFFÉ VITTORIA
290–296 Hanover Street; tel: 617-227-7606; www.vittoriacaffe.com; daily 7am–midnight; $
A quintessential Italian café, with quirky decor that includes almost a museum's worth of antique espresso machines. All kinds of other beverages are also served, along with traditional sweets.

③ THE DAILY CATCH
323 Hanover Street; tel: 617-523-8567; www.dailycatch.com; daily 11am–10pm; $
Cash only at this hole-in-the-wall institution that specializes in Sicilian seafood. The branch at Fan Pier, 2 Northern Avenue (tel: 617-772-4400) is handy for Route 10.

④ SORELLE BAKERY AND CAFÉ
100 City Square, Charlestown; tel: 617-242-5980; www.sorellecafe.com; Mon–Fri 7am–4pm, Sat–Sun 8am–4pm; $
The original is at 1 Monument Avenue, but this branch keeps longer hours and still serves incredible breads and pastries, plus fresh sandwiches and salads.

HARVARD

World-famous Harvard University is actually in the separate city of Cambridge, which lies on the north bank of the Charles River. This walking route takes you around the university's hallowed halls, into some of its excellent museums, and back across the river for fantastic views.

DISTANCE: 4 miles (6.5km)
TIME: A full day including museum visits
START/END: Harvard Square T Station
POINTS TO NOTE: It is difficult to do full justice to all of Harvard's museums in one day. Decide whether you would prefer a brief once-over of everything, or a concentrated session at, say, the natural history museums.

HARVARD YARD

Emerging from **Harvard T Station**, orientate yourself in **Harvard Square ❶**, which is actually an amorphous area rather than a four-sided square. To the west lies the Coop, or Harvard Cooperative Society (a bookstore and department store founded in 1882) which can be interesting to browse. To the east **Harvard Yard** has the university's most historic buildings, bordered on the south and west by Massachusetts Avenue. The Yard is

the geographic heart of America's oldest and most prestigious university, founded in 1636. Six of Harvard's graduates have become US President, and it has churned out dozens of Nobel and Pulitzer prize-winners.

Enter Harvard Yard by the Johnston Gate, on the west arm of Massachusetts Avenue. To the right inside the gate is **Massachusetts Hall** (1718). To the left is **Harvard Hall**. This is the third version of the building, dating from 1766; the original, built in 1642, collapsed, and its 1682 replacement was razed by a fire in 1764. The inferno destroyed the largest library in the colonies, including John Harvard's own collection of books.

Immediately ahead across the grass is **University Hall**, a white granite building designed by Charles Bulfinch in 1814. The bronze statue of John Harvard in front of University Hall is nicknamed 'The Statue of Three Lies', because it is not of John Harvard, but of an 1884 undergraduate sculpted by Daniel French Chester; the inscription refers to John Harvard

as founder of Harvard College, when he was in fact only the first major benefactor; and, contrary to the inscription, the college was not founded in 1638, the year of Harvard's bequest, but in 1636.

NEW YARD

Walk around University Hall into the Tercentenary Quadrangle, or **New Yard ❷**, which, on the last Thursday of each May, is the scene of Com-

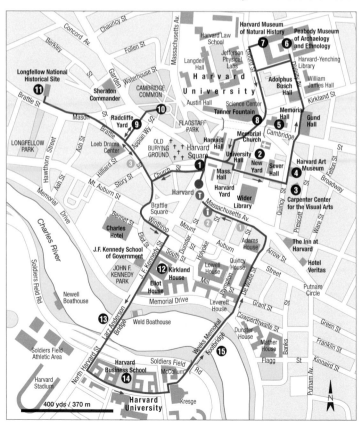

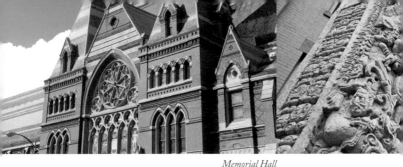

Memorial Hall

mencement, Harvard's major graduation ceremony.

New Yard is dominated on the south by the **Widener Memorial Library** (closed to general public), with its grand Corinthian colonnade atop a monumental flight of stairs. Inside lie 56 miles (90km) of shelves, the third-largest library in the country and part of the largest university library in the world (13 million volumes). The Memorial Room, an elegant affair of wood paneling and stained-glass windows, contains Harry Widener's collection of rare books, including a Gutenberg Bible and a First Folio of Shakespeare.

The northern side of New Yard is punctuated by the soaring, delicate white spire of **Memorial Church**, which honors the Harvard dead in both world wars.

Harvard tours

For the inside scoop on Harvard, take one of the student-led tours of the campus (Feb–Apr and mid-Sept–mid-Dec Mon–Fri 11am and 3pm, Sat 3pm, mid-June–mid-Aug Mon–Sat 11am), leaving from the Harvard University Information Center, Holyoke Center Arcade (1350 Massachusetts Avenue; tel: 617-495-1573; www.harvard.edu). An alternative are the tailor-made Harvard tours (tel: 855-455-8747; www.trademarktours.com/harvard-tour; half- or full-day tours to individual specification). Advance reservations are essential.

On the eastern side of the Yard is the Romanesque **Sever Hall**, considered one of architect H.H. Richardson's finest works. Its entrance is flanked by turreted towers, and the entire building is wonderfully rich in decorative brickwork.

ART MUSEUMS

Walk behind Sever Hall to emerge on Quincy Street, where you will find yourself facing the strikingly modern **Carpenter Center for the Visual Arts** ❸ (www.ves.fas.harvard.edu; exhibitions: Sept–May Mon–Sat 10am–11pm, Sun 1–11pm; admin office: all year Mon–Fri 9am–5pm), the only Le Corbusier building in North America. The ground-floor and third-floor galleries host exhibitions by international artists.

Harvard Art Museum

Next door at no. 32 is the **Harvard Art Museum** ❹ which consists of the **Fogg Art Museum**, the **Busch-Reisinger Museum**, and the **Arthur M. Sackler Museum**. The three museums were combined under one roof into a new building, designed by Renzo Piano, in 2014.

The highlights of the Fogg include works by Ingres, and a fine collection of French Impressionist and Pre-Raphaelite works. In addition, there are dozens of Blake watercolors, and hundreds of Dürer and Rembrandt prints.

Peabody Museum   *On the steps of Widener Library*

The Busch-Reisinger collection, specializing in German art, includes 20th-century Expressionist canvases by Klee and Kandinsky, as well as the archives of architects Gropius and Feininger, forming the largest Bauhaus collection outside Germany.

An outstanding collection of Chinese jades is on display at the Arthur M. Sackler Museum. The Sackler's Ancient and Islamic collections are also noteworthy.

Lunch options

Walk down Quincy Street to Massachusetts Avenue for lunch. Turn right to find **Mr Bartley's Burger Cottage**, see ❶, or walk further down the avenue toward Harvard Square and turn left on Holyoke Street to find **Clover**, see ❷.

MEMORIAL HALL

Return to Quincy Street and follow it north across Cambridge Street. On the left is **Memorial Hall** ❺, a huge, redbrick Victorian Gothic pile, dating from 1874, with polychromatic roofs, which contains the Sanders Theater, the university's largest auditorium. Its somewhat truncated appearance is the result of a fire that destroyed the tall pinnacled roof over the central tower. If the building is open, pop in to admire the stained-glass windows.

On the right of Memorial Hall is the contrasting slender-pillared **Gund Hall**, built in 1969, and home of the Graduate School of Design.

PEABODY MUSEUM

Cross Kirkland Street and enter Divinity Avenue. This is flanked on the left side by the handsome, medieval-style **Adolphus Busch Hall** (named after the beer baron) and on the other by the William James Hall skyscraper, home to the Center of European Studies.

Toward the end of the avenue, on the left at no. 11, is the fascinating **Peabody Museum of Archaelogy and Ethnology** ❻ (www.peabody.harvard.edu; daily 9am–5pm). Among its superb collection of artefacts from around the globe are the only surviving Native American objects gathered by the explorers Meriwether Lewis and William Clark, who led the first American overland expedition to the Pacific coast (1804–6), as well as a huge photographic archive.

MUSEUM OF NATURAL HISTORY

Leaving the Peabody, turn right and right again to follow the footpath around the building to Oxford Street. Here, turn right once more to reach the entrance of the **Harvard Museum of Natural History** ❼ (www.hmnh.harvard.edu; daily 9am–5pm). Its most famous exhibit is the collection of about 4,000 extraordinarily lifelike handmade glass flowers. Kids will also love its collection of dino-

Harvard Business School

saur remains, including a 12ft (3.5m) tall Plateosaurus.

TANNER FOUNTAIN

Exit back onto Oxford Street, and, turning left, continue past the Science Center, the largest building on Harvard campus. In front of it, amid a patch of grass to the north of Harvard Yard, stands the unusual **Tanner Fountain** ❽, gurgling amid a circular grouping of 159 boulders – it's a lovely place to rest and take in the passing scene of students during term time.

Re-enter Harvard Yard. After passing Holworthy, Hollis, Stoughton, and Thayer – all freshman dormitories – you will be back by the Johnston Gate.

RADCLIFFE YARD

Cross Massachusetts Avenue and head west on Church Street. Turn right at the junction with Brattle Street. Continue walking until you pass Appian Way. Next on the right is **Radcliffe Yard** ❾, which is surrounded by a number of delightful late 19th- and early 20th century buildings. This is where the renowned women's college of that name, now fully integrated with Harvard, began life in 1879.

Exit from the yard's far side onto Garden Street, which borders **Cambridge Common** ❿. Surrounded by a semicircle of cannons, a bronze relief marks the spot where, on July 4, 1775, George Washington assumed command of the Continental Army.

LONGFELLOW HOUSE

Return through Radcliffe Yard to Brattle Street, and turn right to see why this is Cambridge's most prestigious street. Leafy and tranquil compared to busy Harvard Square, it is lined by splendid clapboard houses fronted by elegant porticoes, most from the 19th century, some from even earlier. Many bear blue plaques commemorating the great names who lived in them.

The most famous is the cream-colored clapboard building at no. 105, where Henry Wadsworth Longfellow composed many of his most famous works. It is now the **Longfellow National Historical Site** ⓫ (www.nps.gov/long; June–Oct, tours 10am–4pm on the hour, vistitor center 9.30am–5pm). Even if the house is closed, its pleasant grounds are always open for inspection.

Stroll back along Brattle Street toward Harvard Square, perhaps pausing at **L.A. Burdick Chocolate Shop and Café**, see ❸.

TOWARD THE CHARLES RIVER

From Winthrop Street turn right onto John F. Kennedy Street, and walk south past, on the left, the neo-Georgian **Kirkland House** ⓬ and **Eliot House**. Each residential co-ed house is a small college with about 400 students, and herein lies much of Harvard's strength: each house has its own administration

Weeks Memorial Footbridge

Graduation day

and a veritable phalanx of tutors; its own library and dining hall; and its own exclusive societies and clubs.

On the other side of John F. Kennedy Street, facing Kirkland and Eliot houses, is Harvard's **John F. Kennedy School of Government** (www.hks.harvard.edu), fronted by the riverside John F. Kennedy Park.

Across busy Memorial Drive the handsome **Larz Anderson Bridge ⑬**, named in memory of Nicholas Longworth Anderson, a distinguished colonel in the US Civil War, spans the Charles River.

HARVARD BUSINESS SCHOOL

Cross the river, and continue straight on what is now North Harvard Street for 100yds/m, passing on the right the Harvard playing fields and, on the left, the prestigious **Harvard Business School ⑭**. Turn left and stroll through the campus. Here the neo-Georgian buildings display a consistent rhythm of green doors, white window-frames, and red-brick walls.

Emerging on the school's eastern side, take the footbridge over busy Soldiers Field Road that leads to the **Weeks Memorial Footbridge ⑮**, which again offers an excellent view of some of Harvard's residential buildings.

Cross Memorial Drive and head north along DeWolfe Street aiming for Massachusetts Avenue, where a left turn will bring you back to Harvard Square.

Food and drink

① MR BARTLEY'S BURGER COTTAGE

1246 Massachusetts Avenue; tel: 617-354-6559; www.bartleysburgers.com; Mon–Sat 11am–9pm; $

A Harvard institution, this classic mom-and-pop burger joint offers a wide range of burgers named after famous politicians like Bill Clinton and Arnold Schwarzenegger ('this is no girly burger'). Wash them down with a raspberry lime rickey or a thick frappe.

② CLOVER

7 Holyoke Street; www.cloverfoodlab.com; daily 7am–10pm; $

This hip veggie operation, which started as a food truck at MIT, serves local, organic produce, from its permanent Harvard base. From granola and yoghurt for breakfast to a chickpea fritter plate for lunch or dinner, it's all good.

③ L.A. BURDICK CHOCOLATE SHOP AND CAFÉ

52-D Brattle Street; tel: 617-491-4340; www.burdickchocolate.com; Sun–Thu 8am–8pm, Fri–Sat 8am–10pm; $

A quiet oasis removed from the bustle of Harvard Square. Indulge in delectable handmade chocolates and pastries, accompanied by a great range of teas and coffees. Their hot chocolate is like dessert in a cup.

CHARLES RIVER AND MIT

Experience both the relaxed and scientific side of Boston on this loop walk along the banks of the Charles River and through the campus of Massachusetts Institute of Technology (MIT), home to some of the nation's most innovative thinkers and eye-catching architecture.

DISTANCE: 5.5 miles (8.5km)
TIME: A full day including museum visits
START/END: Charles/MGH T Station
POINTS TO NOTE: If you plan to eat at 'The Trucks' on MIT campus, do this route on a weekday. An early-morning tour of the Museum of Science is a good idea to avoid the crowds of schoolchildren that can descend on the place later in the day. MIT tours run throughout the year, but a visit during term time is recommended to experience the student atmosphere.

Although the fast-moving traffic of Storrow Drive to the south and Memorial Drive to the north seems to isolate the Charles River from the city, pedestrian bridges over these highways mean that this riverside walk is easy to access. The route is popular with joggers, and, if you have a bicycle, it also makes for a very pleasant ride, with a dedicated cycle path most of the way. If you get tired, there are several points where you can exit the walk and hop back on the T. You may wish to extend the walk along the river to connect with part of the Harvard route.

LONGFELLOW BRIDGE

Exit Charles/MGH T Station on the Beacon Hill (southern) side and walk right toward the pedestrian bridge over Storrow Drive. On the other side turn right and head under the handsome **Longfellow Bridge**, often referred to as the Salt and Pepper Shaker Bridge, after the distinctive shape of its towers.

On the northern side of the bridge you will pass **Teddy Ebersol's Red Sox Fields ❶**, named after a young Red Sox fan who died in a plane crash. Here young athletes train in softball and soccer as well as baseball. Head past the kids' playground and the tennis courts to turn left from Storrow Drive onto the Charles River Dam. A metal grill here crosses the river at its narrowest point.

MUSEUM OF SCIENCE

Perched on Charles River Dam, with a life-sized model of a T rex out-

Longfellow Bridge

side, is the interactive and educational **Museum of Science** ❷ (www.mos.org; Sat–Thu 9am–5pm, Fri 9am–9pm, July–Labor Day Sat–Thu 9am–7pm), which boasts 600-plus exhibits in six major fields: astronomy, computing, energy, anthropology, industry, and nature.

Also here are the **Charles Hayden Planetarium**, offering excellent programs on astronomy, plus laser light shows, and the **Mugar Omni Theater**, where IMAX movies are projected onto a giant high-domed screen. As you leave the Museum of Science, take note of the small garden bordered by rock samples, some quite beautiful, from throughout the world, including pieces from the Grand Canyon, Giant's Causeway in Northern Ireland, and Mont Blanc.

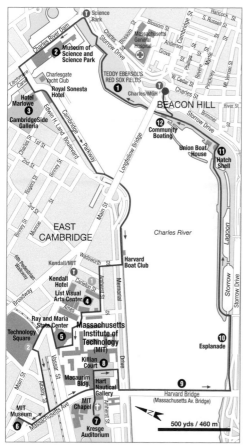

EATING OPTIONS

Turn left on leaving the museum and, at the end of the bridge, turn left again onto Edwin H. Land Boulevard, which crosses the narrow Lechmere Canal. To the right is the large shopping mall **CambridgeSide Galleria** ❸ (www.cambridgesidegalleria.com).

Frank Gehry's Stata Center

Continue heading south along the river toward the Longfellow Bridge; the view here of the bridge with the city skyline behind is one of the best on the walk. Pass under the bridge and you will be walking alongside Memorial Drive. Cross this highway just after passing the Harvard Boat Club, walk down Wadsworth Street, and turn left on Amherst Street to enter the MIT campus. On the right at Carleton Street you will find **'The Trucks'**, see ❶.

MIT

Massachusetts Institute of Technology (MIT) was founded in 1861, and has been based here since 1916. Its reputation for science research obscures the fact that there is a fair amount of support for the arts on campus too.

List Visual Arts Center
Turn right at the end of Amherst Street to arrive at the **List Visual Arts Center** ❹ (Wiesner Building, 20 Ames Street; http://listart.mit.edu; daily noon–6pm; Thu until 8pm), which features temporary exhibits of superb contemporary art.

Ray and Maria Stata Center
Cross Ames Street and walk toward the whimsical **Ray and Maria Stata Center** ❺ (self-guided tour leaflet available from the information desk), a Frank Gehry building that is home to MIT's computer science and artificial intelligence lab. Detour over one street west

to Main St to find **Area Four**, see ❷, a cool lunch or coffee spot.

MIT MUSEUM

From Main Street, head south down Albany Street to Massachusetts Avenue where you should hang a right to reach, at no. 265, the fascinating **MIT Museum** ❻ (http://web.mit.edu/museum; daily 10am–5pm), which showcases the institute's history, scientific advances, and inventions, as well as the latter's artistic applications; check out the world's largest collection of holographic images. Part of the museum's collection is displayed back on the main campus in the **Hart Nautical Museum** (55 Massachusetts Avenue; same hours; free last Sun of each month).

MIT WEST CAMPUS

Walk back along Massachusetts Avenue toward the river. Before entering the heart of MIT, through the grand portico on the left, take a moment to look at a couple of buildings on the western side of the campus. The **Kresge Auditorium** ❼ and the **MIT Chapel** facing it are two buildings designed by a Finnish architect, Eero Saarinen. The auditorium, completed in 1953, is an enormous tent-like structure rising out of a circular brick terrace. Two years later Saarinen designed the tiny multi-faith chapel, which is best appreciated from

Maclaurin Building at MIT　　　　　　　*Sail-boats on the Charles River*

inside; there are no windows, but light floods in from the ceiling, bouncing off a hanging sculpture by Harry Bertola behind the altar.

MIT East Campus

From MIT's main entrance walk along the central hallway of the domed Maclaurin Building, known as 'The Infinite Corridor': weather permitting, the sun shines directly into the corridor twice a year. Exit the Maclaurin Building into grassy **Killian Court ❽** facing the river. At the southern end is a sculpture by Henry Moore (right) and another by Michael Heizer (left).

HARVARD BRIDGE

Exit from the court and turn right along Memorial Drive. On the left is **Harvard Bridge ❾** (also known as Massachusetts Avenue Bridge), the longest bridge across the Charles, which provides sweeping views both up and down the river. At the bridge's end follow the footpath off to the left to reach the **Esplanade ❿** (www.esplanadeassociation. org), a riverside park designed by Frederick Law Olmstead. The idyllic Storrow Lagoon, spanned by four small-arched stone bridges, extends for about a mile (nearly 2km).

BOSTON POPS

Beyond the lagoon is the **Hatch Shell ⓫** (www.hatchshell.com), where free

outdoor concerts, anchored by the Boston Pops Esplanade Orchestra, are held May to September. The highlight is the July 4 concert and fireworks display.

Behind the Shell is the boathouse of the Union Boat Club – the US's oldest rowing club, founded in 1851. Some 300yds/m beyond is the clubhouse of **Community Boating ⓬** (www.community-boating.org), a public sailing program. Next to here is the footbridge back over the highway to Charles/MGH T Station.

Food and drink

❶ 'THE TRUCKS'

Carleton Street, MIT Campus; Mon–Fri 10.30am–4pm (hours may vary); $
Near the Kendall/MIT T Station, these food trucks are an MIT institution. Join throngs of students and alumni working in the area for lunch. Popular ones include Saté Grill for light Asian dishes and The Chicken and Rice Guys.

❷ AREA FOUR

500 Technology Square; tel: 617-758-4444; www.areafour.com; Mon–Fri 7am–10pm, Sat–Sun 8am–10pm; $$
Area Four covers all bases from bakery/café to bar and restaurant. Portions can be small but the ingredients are local and fresh; opt for gourmet pizza, home-made ice creams, and New England ales.

Row houses on Beacon Hill

BEACON HILL AND THE PUBLIC GARDEN

Packed with historic buildings, and the location of the Black Heritage Trail, Beacon Hill is one of Boston's most exclusive neighborhoods. A stroll here allows a glimpse into Boston's genteel past and elegant present.

DISTANCE: 3 miles (5km)
TIME: A half day
START: Park Street T Station
END: Arlington Street T Station
POINTS TO NOTE: If you want to tour the State House, do this route on a weekday. You can easily extend the route by browsing the many shops along Charles Street.

The enchanting traffic-free streets of Beacon Hill are a delightful place to explore on foot. The most unswervingly traditional of all Boston's neighborhoods, the Hill has long been associated with wealthy 'Boston Brahmins' – the self-deprecating term coined by Oliver Wendell Holmes for the city's most illustrious families. However, Beacon Hill has always attracted a diverse population, with bohemian types residing on the north or 'bad' side – the derogatory term refers to the social standing of the residents rather than its contrast with the sunnier south side.

ROBERT GOULD SHAW MEMORIAL

This route starts at **Park Street Station** at the northeastern corner of Boston Common. Head uphill through the park toward the Massachusetts State House. Immediately opposite this august institution pause to admire the **Shaw 54th Regiment Memorial ❶**, honoring the first regiment of freed blacks in the Civil War. Their leader was 26-year-old white officer Robert Gould Shaw. The relief, sculpted by Augustus Saint Gaudens, depicts the regiment's farewell march down Beacon Street.

MASSACHUSETTS STATE HOUSE

At the crest of Beacon Street is the **Massachusetts State House ❷** (www.sec. state.ma.us; Mon–Fri 10am–3:30pm), designed by Beacon Hill's pre-eminent architect Charles Bulfinch and completed in 1798. Dubbed 'the Hub of the Solar System' by Oliver Wendell Holmes, this regal building's most visually impressive feature, the glittering

Massachusetts State House

dome crowned in golf leaf in 1861, was originally covered with shingles.

Take one of the 45-minute tours here to see the Doric Hall – a vaulted, columned marble hall with a statue of Washington – and the Hall of Flags, which displays the colors of state military units. A double stairway climbs to the chamber of the House of Representatives, an impressive oval room in which hangs the Sacred Cod, a gilded, carved-wood representation of the staple diet of the first settlers in the region and later a mainstay of both Boston's and the state's economy.

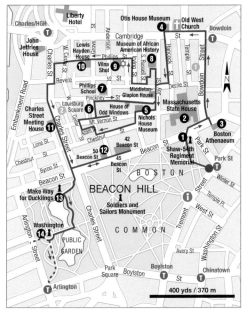

BOSTON ATHENAEUM

A short way further east down Beacon Street is the **Boston Athenaeum** ❸ (www.bostonathenaeum.org; Wed–Sat 10am–4pm, Tue noon–8pm), a private library founded in 1807. The building was restored and sensitively extended in 1999; it's well worth signing up for one of the tours (Tue 5:30pm, Thu 3pm, and Sun 11am) otherwise the library hosts art shows that are open to the public. The library's half a million volumes – browsed by the likes of Ralph Waldo Emerson and Nathaniel Hawthorne – are off limits to all but members.

Since the State House gardens are not accessible by the public, you will have to peer through the front railings to view the statues of famous Bostonians. From left to right they are: the religious martyr Anne Hutchinson, President John F. Kennedy, educator Horace Mann, Civil War general Joseph Hooker, and another religious martyr, Mary Dyer.

Backtrack to turn right on Bowdoin Street, where you will walk past the side of the State

Acorn Street

House to reach **Grotto**, see ①, a fine lunch option.

OTIS HOUSE MUSEUM

Before heading into the heart of Beacon Hill, continue down Bowdoin Street until you reach Cambridge Street. A short distance to the left at no. 141 is the **Otis House Museum** ④ (www.historicnewengland.org; Wed–Sun 11am–5pm), the first of three homes in the area that Bulfinch designed in 1796 for Harrison Gray Otis, a real-estate developer turned politician. Today it is owned by the preservation body Historic New England, which has recreated the interior according to how it would have been at the turn of the 19th century.

NICHOLS HOUSE MUSEUM

Hike back up Hancock Street, turn right on Derne Street, then at the junction with Joy Street turn left and walk two blocks to Mount Vernon Street to enter the heart of the area. Here the tree-lined streets are narrower and bordered by elegant blocks of red-brick townhouses, enhanced by wrought-iron railings, window boxes of flowers, slender columns flanking doorways, delicate fanlights, and quirky brass door knockers.

Few of these homes are open to the public; one exception is the **Nichols House Museum** ⑤ (55 Mount Vernon Street; www.nicholshousemuseum.org; 11am–4pm Apr–Oct Tue–Sat, Nov– Mar Thu–Sat), which is well worth a visit. Inside this 1804 house, attributed to Bulfinch, is preserved the daily life of author and suffragette Ms Rose Standish Nichols, resident from 1885 to 1960.

SOUTH SLOPE STREETS

Turn left down Walnut Street, then right onto **Chestnut Street** where nos 13, 15, 17, and 29a provide further examples of Bulfinch's work; the latter is the oldest home on the South slope. Take the first right onto Willow Street and turn immediately left onto cobbled **Acorn Street**, one of Beacon Hill's most picturesque and most photographed streets. Acorn ends in West Cedar Street, where in the 1950s furious residents sat down on the walkway to save the Hill's brick sidewalks from demolition. A right turn here leads back to Mount Vernon Street.

Henry James claimed **Mount Vernon Street** was 'the only respectable street in America.' Glancing up at no. 85, the free-standing **Second Harrison Gray Otis House** (1800), it is difficult to disagree. This Bulfinch building represents his vision of Mount Vernon Street, which he hoped would be lined by mansions, each in its own spacious grounds. Back at no. 88, fronting Louisburg Square, a plaque notes that the poet and Pulitzer Prize-winner Robert Lee Frost lived here from 1938 to 1941 while teaching at Harvard.

Louisburg Square   *Staircase in Nichols House Museum*

No such plaque commemorates Louisa May Alcott, who lived in **Louisburg Square** ❻ (the 's' is pronounced) at no. 10. Her literary success with *Little Women* allowed her to move to this sort after address.

The square's dignified red-brick row of houses, among the most expensive in Boston, includes, at the northeast corner, the home of former presidential candidate Senator John Kerry. In the centre is a small iron-fenced residents' park.

NORTH SLOPE STREETS

Exiting from the northern side of the square, turn right onto **Pinckney Street**, the dividing line between the posh South Slope and the less desirable North Slope. As well as aspiring writers, such as Louisa May Alcott, who lived at no. 20 with her family before she struck it rich, the street was home in the 19th century to a large and thriving African American community.

The red-brick condominium building at the corner of Anderson Street was once the **Phillips School** ❼, which, when opened to African Americans in 1855, became the city's first interracial school. Across the street at no. 62 is one of several houses that were used as stopovers on the 'Underground Railroad' traveled by fugitive slaves on their way to freedom north of the border in Canada.

At no. 24 is the aptly named **House of Odd Windows**, designed by a nephew of Ralph Waldo Emerson.

MUSEUM OF AFRICAN AMERICAN HISTORY

Turn left onto Joy Street, walk downhill and you will arrive at Smith Court and the **Museum of African American History** ❽ (www.maah.org; Mon–Sat 10am–4pm), housed in the Abiel Smith School, and dedicated in 1834 to the education of the city's African American children. Adjacent is the African Meeting House, the nation's oldest African American church. The museum's displays chart the contribution

Underground Railroad

Beacon Hill was a key stop on the Underground Railroad, an informal network of secret routes and safe houses used by black slaves before the US Civil War to escape the southern US for the northern free states and Canada. Here the runaway slaves found many abolitionists and former slaves who were sympathetic to their cause.

You can find out more about the route while following the Black Heritage Trail. Starting at the Robert Gould Shaw Memorial and running through Beacon Hill, the trail explores the history of Boston's 19th-century African American community. Go to www.maah.org for a map and a self-guided tour of the trail's 14 sites or contact the National Park Service (see page 131) about its daily free guided tours.

Swan boats

African Americans made to New England from Colonial times through to the 19th century.

At one time all the houses in Smith Court were occupied by African Americans. Also known as 'Black Faneuil Hall', the African Meeting House hosted anti-slavery meetings that culminated in 1832 with the founding of William Lloyd Garrison's New England Anti-Slavery Society.

Smith Court leads into narrow **Holmes Alley**, one of the 'secret' passageways along which fugitive slaves could escape from their pursuers – follow its twists south then west to emerge on South Russell Street.

VILNA SHUL AND LEWIS HAYDEN HOUSE

At South Russell Street turn left, then right onto Myrtle Street, right again down Irving Street, and left onto Phillips Street. At no. 16 stands the **Vilna Shul** ❾, (www.vilnashul. org; mid-March–mid-Nov Wed–Fri 11am–5pm, Sun 1–5pm) one of the remaining synagogues of the many that once stood in the area. Now a museum, it dates from 1919 but was founded much earlier in a different location in the now demolished West End. Inside you can find out about how the pews were once part of a Baptist church and how the synagogue inspired Leonard Nimoy to create his Vulcan salute in *Star Trek*.

At no. 66 Philips Street stands **Lewis Hayden House** ❿, a private residence that was a famous refuge for runaway slaves. The house was owned by Hayden, a former slave, who threatened to blow up anyone who dared try to search it – no one ever did.

At the end of Philips Street look for Putnam Avenue, a private lane that connects to Charles Street, Beacon Hill's commercial hub.

CHARLES STREET

Lined with antiques shops, galleries, high-end specialty shops, and eateries, Charles Street is a pleasure to browse. A few hundred yards along on the left, near The Hungry I, see ❷, is the former **Charles Street Meeting House** ⓫, now a complex of offices and stores. Recognizable by its lantern tower and clock, it was bought by the African Methodist Episcopalian Church in 1939.

BEACON STREET

Turn left at the junction of Charles and Beacon streets. Facing Boston Common are some of the grandest Beacon Hill buildings. At **no. 50** ⓬, on the corner of Spruce Street, a plaque commemorates Rev. Blackstone, the original Bostonian, who came to live at this spot – then known as Shawmut by the Native Americans – in 1625.

The Federal-style building at **no. 45** is the third house built by Bulfinch

Public Garden's formal flowerbeds

for Harrison Gray Otis, who lived here from 1806 until his death in 1848. It is now occupied by the American Meteorological Society (www.ametsoc.org), and if you get in touch in advance it is sometimes possible to arrange tours of its interior.

Almost next door, at **no. 42**, the glistening white granite building with two large bow windows belongs to the exclusive Somerset Club. The attitude of this establishment's members can be seen from the time the club caught fire, and firefighters were told to use the tradesmen's entrance – marked by a handsome pair of lion door handles.

THE PUBLIC GARDEN

Retrace your steps back downhill to the corner of Charles and Beacon streets, where you can enter the glorious **Public Garden**, the oldest botanical garden in the US. Although not large, it has magnificently maintained formal flower beds and a lovely lagoon, bordered by weeping willows, on which float the famous Swan Boats.

Close by the Charles Street entrance is the charming ***Make Way for Ducklings*** sculpture ⓭, based on the characters in the classic American children's book of the same name by Robert McCloskey (first published in 1941) – it is always a hit with the little ones.

Head from here toward the miniature suspension bridge over the lagoon. Ahead you will see a splendid equestrian **statue of Washington** ⓮. The first president was also, according to Jefferson, the finest horseman of the age.

Emerge from the garden here at the foot of Commonwealth Avenue where you can start Route 6, or you can continue south to the corner of Arlington and Boylston streets, where you will find the Arlington T stop.

Food and drink

❶ GROTTO

37 Bowdoin Street; tel: 617-227-3434; www.grottorestaurant.com; lunch Mon–Fri 11.30am–3pm, dinner daily 5–10pm; $$
The basement location of this boho-chic Italian restaurant might be off-putting on a sunny day, but the food is well worth it. Salads, pastas, and sandwiches are all made with top-grade ingredients.

❷ THE HUNGRY I

71 Charles Street; tel: 617-227-3524; www.hungryiboston.com; lunch Thu–Fri noon–2pm, dinner Sun–Thu 5.30pm–9.30pm, Fri–Sat until 10pm, brunch Sun 11am–2pm; $$$
This charming, romantic restaurant is situated in the basement of a brownstone. The open fireplace and traditional décor help create a cozy atmosphere for winter and evening dining with a vine-covered terrace for summer lunching.

Boston Public Library and New Old South Church

BACK BAY

Back Bay, with its neat grid pattern and alphabetical progression of the cross streets from Arlington to Hereford, is bisected by the grand boulevard of Commonwealth Avenue. Around it there are historic mansions and churches, and the choice shopping precincts of Newbury Street and Copley Place.

DISTANCE: 3.5 miles (5.5km)
TIME: A half day
START: Arlington T Station
END: Symphony T Station
POINTS TO NOTE: You may wish to allow time to browse Back Bay's many shops. If you walk the route after lunch, you could end with a sunset drink at the Top of the Hub.

Originally a shallow estuary, Back Bay was filled in and laid out by mid-Victorian believers in the urban grid pattern, eager to make expansive use of 'made land' and put Downtown's tortuous alleys and the narrow streets of Beacon Hill behind them. This was Boston's most exclusive address until the Great Depression of the 1930s saw aristocratic homes converted into apartments and college dormitories. It has now regained its former glory, and is home to Boston's new wealth.

COMMONWEALTH AVENUE

From Arlington T Station walk north on Arlington Street, passing the brownstone **Arlington Street Church** ❶ (www.asc boston.org), considered to be the 'mother church' of Unitarianism in the US, and one of first buildings to rise in Back Bay in 1861. Continue past the east end of Newbury Street – there will be a chance to trawl its boutiques later – and the Taj Boston (formerly the Ritz-Carlton and still something of an institution).

The next corner leads to the foot of **Commonwealth Avenue**, Back Bay's pièce de résistance. Commonly known as Com Ave, this French-inspired boulevard has a 100ft (30m) wide strip of park adorned by statues running down its middle, the first you'll encounter is of Alexander Hamilton, first Treasury Secretary under President Washington. Magnificent buildings, many once single family homes, line either side of the street.

BEACON STREET

Gibson House Museum

Turn right on Berkeley Street, walk to the corner of Beacon Street, and

Trinity Church's apse

turn right again to arrive at no. 137, the **Gibson House Museum** ❷ (www. thegibsonhouse.org; tours Wed–Sun 1, 2 and 3pm). This 1860 Italian Renaissance-style row house from the first period of Back Bay construction comes complete with original Victorian furnishings, preserved intact through the tenure of the last owner, a scion of the Gibson family who died in the 1950s.

Isabella Stewart Gardner's home

Continue west along Beacon Street, where on the right side you will pass **no. 150**. On this spot once stood the home of Isabella Stewart Gardner, Boston's most famous private art collector, before she moved to the Fenway (see page 69). Mrs Gardner actually lived at no. 152, but when she moved the eccentric heiress insisted that the number never be used again on the street. Her wish has been respected.

Goethe Institute

A little further along, at no. 170, it is possible to look inside the **Goethe Institute** ❸ (www. goethe.de/boston;

Mon–Fri 9am–3pm), a German cultural center based in a 1901 home. On the ground floor is the former ballroom with beautiful moulding decoration, while the library upstairs has a balcony that provides glimpses across to the Charles River.

BACK ON COMMONWEALTH AVENUE

From the Goethe Institute turn left onto Clarendon Street and return to

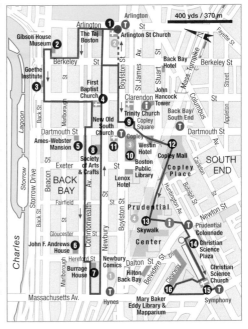

The Library's colonnaded courtyard

Commonwealth Avenue, where you will note the **First Baptist Church** ❹ (www.firstbaptistchurchofboston. com), dating from the early 1870s, and affectionately known as the 'Church of the Holy Bean Blowers' after the trumpeting angels at the corners of its tower. The faces of the frieze (modeled by Auguste Batholdi, sculptor of the Statue of Liberty) that decorate the top of the church's tower are said to be likenesses of notable Bostonians, such as Longfellow, Emerson, and Hawthorne.

Notable mansions

Continue down the spine of Commonwealth Avenue to the intersection with Dartmouth Street. The grand corner building on the right-hand side is the **Ames-Webster Mansion** ❺ (306 Dartmouth Street), dating from 1872. Much of its elaborate interior design, including a grand hall with carved-oak panels, 18ft (5.5m) -high ceilings, and stained-glass windows, was preserved when the building was turned into commercial offices later in its life.

Head further down the avenue to the intersection with Hereford Street. On the right is **John F. Andrews House** ❻ (32 Hereford Street), Back Bay's first Italian Renaissance Revival-style building, now well maintained by an MIT fraternity. On the opposite side, at 314 Commonwealth Avenue, ornamentation runs riot at the flamboyant **Burrage House** ❼, built in 1899, a synthesis of Vanderbilt-style mansion and French chateau.

SHOPPING ON NEWBURY STREET

Turn left off Commonwealth Avenue at Massachusetts Avenue and walk a block to **Newbury Street**, Back Bay's most eclectic shopping destination. At this end of Newbury the vibe is studenty and hip, as typified by the clientele of **Trident Booksellers and Café**, see ❶, next door to which you will find Newbury Comics (www.newburycom ics.com), one of Boston's best music, video, and comic stores.

Further down Newbury you can browse antiques stores and art galleries, including, at No. 175, the **Society of Arts & Crafts** ❽ (www.societyofcrafts.org; Tue–Sat 10am–6pm, Thursday until 9pm), which dates back to 1897 and represents over 400 artists from across the US; and at No. 167, **DTR Modern Galleries** (www.dtrmodern.com; Mon–Sat 10am–6pm, Sun noon–6pm) which exhibits pieces from such 20th and 21st century luminaries as Salvador Dali, Marc Chagall, Damien Hirst and Anish Kapoor.

Newbury Street also has plenty of appealing cafés and restaurants, some with street-side dining in the warmer months. The closer you get to Arlington Street the more upmarket the stores become, featuring the likes

Bates Hall reading room in the Public Library

of Giorgio Armani, Brookes Brothers, and the jewelers Shreve, Crump & Low at No. 39.

COPLEY SQUARE

Turn right at the junction with Arlington, then left onto Boylston Street, where you will hit Arlington T Station, a possible exit point from this walk if you are feeling tired, and the **Parish Café**, see ➋, if you fancy lunch. Back Bay still has plenty more to offer, so, if you wish to continue, head straight down Boylston three blocks to reach **Copley Square ➒**, named after the great Boston painter John Singleton Copley and one of the city's focal points.

Trinity Church
Copley Square's most renowned building, on the eastern side, is **Trinity Church** (www.trinitychurchboston.org; Mon, Fri–Sat 9am–5pm, Tue–Thu 9am–6pm, Sun 7am–7pm), a seminal work in American architecture that initiated the Romanesque revival. Enter through the west porch, which leads into a richly decorated interior. The superb frescoes are the work of John La Farge, who also supervised the stained-glass windows.

Rising up 62 stories behind the church is the I.M. Pei-designed **John Hancock Tower**, with 10,000 panels of mirrored glass reflecting all around it.

Boston Public Library
Facing the western side of Copley Square is the venerable **Boston Public Library ➓** (www.bpl.org; Mon–Thu 9am–9pm, Fri–Sat 9am–5pm), designed by Charles Follen McKim in 1852. The interior of the old wing is spectacular. Climb a grand stairway to the second floor to view one of the library's murals, a painting of the Nine Muses by the Parisian artist Puvis de Chavannes.

On the right is **Bates Hall**, an enormous reading room with a barrel-vaulted ceiling, named after Joshua Bates, the library's first major benefactor. This is a familiar scene form many movies filmed in Boston. An adjoining room displays Pre-Raphaelite murals.

Go up one more floor to see the **John Singer Sargent Gallery**, featuring a series of murals on religious themes.

The lovely Italian-cloistered **courtyard** in the center of the building is one of the city's most peaceful retreats, and you can enjoy it with refreshments from **The Courtyard**, see ➌.

New Old South Church
Opposite the Public Library on the corner of Bolyston and Dartmouth streets is the striking Italian Gothic campanile of the **New Old South Church ⓫** (www.oldsouth.org), dating from 1875. The original Old South still stands Downtown. The church's orig-

New Old South Church

inal 246ft (75m) tower, which began to lean soon after construction, had to be dismantled and rebuilt slightly lower in 1931.

COPLEY PLACE

Head in the other direction toward where Huntington Avenue meets Dartmouth Street at the entrance to the Westin Hotel, which is part of **Copley Place** ⑫, central Boston's largest and glitziest shopping and office complex. Follow the corridors through the building to arrive at two floors of upmarket stores surrounding a nine-story atrium, in the center of which is a 60ft (18m) travertine and granite waterfall sculpture.

PRUDENTIAL CENTER

An enclosed walkway from Copley Mall leads you over Huntington Avenue into the **Prudential Center**, another shopping mall surrounding the 52-story Prudential Tower. On the 50th floor is the **Skywalk** ⑬ (www.skywalkboston. com; daily Apr–Nov 10am–10pm, Dec–Mar 10am–8pm), which provides 360-degree views of the city through floor-to-ceiling windows, as well as the *Dreams of Freedom* exhibition about the history of immigration in Boston. This is an ideal spot to return to at the end of the walk to enjoy a cocktail at the **Top of the Hub**, see ④, the restaurant and bar on the tower's 52nd floor.

Unless you hire a helicopter to fly over the city, the bird's-eye views from either of Prudential's venues are pretty exceptional; the viewing gallery at the top of the nearby John Hancock Tower closed after 9/11.

CHRISTIAN SCIENCE PLAZA

Exit the Prudential Center at the corner of Huntington Avenue and Belvidere Street, across from which lies the 670ft (200m) -long reflecting pool that forms the centerpiece of the **Christian Science Plaza** ⑭, designed by I.M. Pei in the early 1970s and one of the most monumental public spaces in the city.

Christian Science Church
Along the north side of pool runs the five-story Colonnade Building, culminating in the separate **Christian Science Church** ⑮ (http:// christianscience.com; Tue noon–4pm, Wed 1–4pm, Thu–Sat noon–5pm, Sun 11am–3pm), the original church of the movement founded by Mary Baker Eddy (1821–1910) and headquartered in Boston since 1882.

The church is entered through a dramatic basilica-like structure, a mixture of Byzantine and Italian Renaissance styles. As you will discover on the guided tour, this part is the church's 1906 extension that seats 3,000 on three levels. The pipe

On the Christian Science Plaza

organ here is one of the largest in the Western hemisphere.

Tucked behind this is the original Mother Church from 1894, with 82 beautiful stained-glass windows depicting biblical events.

Mary Baker Eddy Library and Mapparium

On leaving the church, immediately to the right, with its entrance at 200 Massachusetts Avenue, is the **Mary Baker Eddy Library and Mapparium** ⑯

(www.marybakereddylibrary.org; Tue–Sun 10am–4pm). The highlight of the beautifully designed interior is the Mapparium (last tour at 3.40pm), a globe 30ft (9m) in diameter, made up of 608 stained-glass panels, and into which you can walk. It provides a snapshot of the world as it was in 1935. The echoing acoustics are uncanny.

Exit from the library onto Massachusetts Avenue. Head southeast along the road and you will eventually come to Symphony T Station.

Food and drink

① TRIDENT BOOKSELLERS AND CAFÉ

338 Newbury Street; tel: 617-267-8688; www.tridentbookscafe.com; daily 8am–midnight; $

The café has expanded and the bookshop shrunk at this convivial place offering simple fare, such as homemade soups, fresh salads, and daily specials. Another plus is their perpetual breakfast.

② PARISH CAFÉ

361 Boylston Street; tel: 617-247-4777; www.parishcafe.com; Mon–Sat 11.30–1am, Sun noon–1am; $$

The menu of sandwiches designed by some of Boston's celebrity chefs is a little gimmicky but nevertheless, it works. There is an extensive list of beers and other drinks, and the outdoor patio complements the experience in the summer.

③ THE COURTYARD

Boston Public Library, 700 Boylston Street; tel: 617-859-2251; www.thecateredaffair.com; lunch Tue–Sat 11.30am–5pm; $

Serves an elaborate lunch including fancy sandwiches, salads, and luscious desserts, as well as a set afternoon tea (Wed–Fri 2–4pm), all with a view of the library courtyard's fountain. Next door the self-serve MapRoom Café is open Mon–Sat 9am–5pm.

④ TOP OF THE HUB

52nd floor, Prudential Tower; tel: 617-536-1775; www.topofthehub.net; Mon–Sat 11.30–1am, Sun 11–1am; $$$

The food is generally overpriced, but this is a romantic place with a phenomenal view for drinks at sundown. After 8pm there is a $24 minimum spend in the lounge but also live jazz. Advance reservation is recommended.

Baseball at Fenway Park

BACK BAY FENS

Beyond Massachusetts Avenue, architecturally dense Back Bay yields to the Fenway, a loose scattering of institutions and apartment buildings joined by the meandering path of the Back Bay Fens, an urban archipelago of parkland.

DISTANCE: 1.25 miles (2km)
TIME: 2 hours
START: Kenmore T Station
END: Longwood Medical Area T Station
POINTS TO NOTE: This route can be combined with Route 8 covering the Museum of Fine Arts and the Isabella Stewart Gardner Museum. Note that the area around Victory Gardens in the Fens is a notorious gay cruising area and also a common site of late-night muggings.

KENMORE SQUARE

Begin at **Kenmore Square ❶**, where Commonwealth Avenue, Brookline Avenue, and Beacon Street meet beneath the gaze of the giant Citgo sign. If you arrive by the T, take the Fenway exit to emerge on the southern side of Commonwealth Avenue. On the northern side of the Square you will find **Uburger**, see ❶, and further west along Commonwealth Avenue lies the sprawling campus of Boston University.

FENWAY PARK

Hang a left into Brookline Avenue and head over the Massachusetts Turnpike for a view of the back of the Green Monster. This is the nickname of the left field wall of **Fenway Park ❷** (www.mlb.com/redsox; tours non-game days: 9am–5pm, game days 3 hours prior to game time), home to the Red Sox baseball team. Built in 1912, Fenway Park is the smallest and oldest stadium in the major leagues.

Walking around the ground's perimeter, turn left into Yawkey Way where you

Food and drink

❶ UBURGER

636 Beacon Street; tel: 617-536-0448; www.uburger.com; Mon–Sat 11am–11pm, Sun noon–11pm; $
This generic-looking café is fêted by Boston burger-lovers. They grind their own prime beef, hand-cut their fries and onion rings, and charge from $4.75 for their burgers. At lunch the line can be out the door.

The long-standing Citgo sign

Clothing for Red Sox fans

will find the official store for Red Sox souvenirs. Turn left at Van Ness Street and walk along the ball park's southern side to encounter a statue of local legend **Ted Williams** ❸ beside Gate B. Turning right will quickly bring you to Bolyston Street across which are the Back Bay Fens.

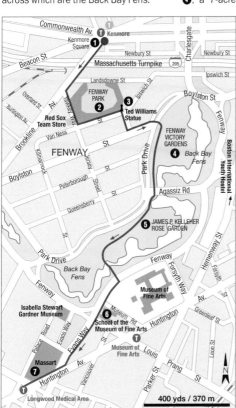

THE BACK BAY FENS

The reedy marshland along the Muddy River is a major link in the Emerald Necklace. Across Park Drive from Boylston Street are the **Fenway Victory Gardens** ❹, a 7-acre (3 hectare) allotment site created in 1942. Further around the Fens, just south from Agassiz Road, is the **James P. Kelleher Rose Garden** ❺, established in 1930.

ART SCHOOLS

A footbridge at the southern end of the Fens will take you across the creek to the Fenway entrance of the **Museum of Fine Arts** (see page 66). Next to it, on the corner of Museum Road and Evans Way, is the **School of the Museum of Fine Arts** ❻ (www.smfa.edu), which hosts exhibitions by students and budding artists.

More contemporary art can be seen in the galleries of nearby **Massart** ❼ (621 Huntington Avenue; https://massart.edu), the Massachusetts College of Art. Hop back on the T at Longwood Medical Area Station.

Museum of Fine Arts

TWO ART MUSEUMS

Exploring the wonderful collections of these two storied museums will take you from Egyptian antiquities to ambitious 21st-century works.

DISTANCE: 0.25 mile (0.5km)
TIME: A full day
START/END: Museum of Fine Arts T Station
POINTS TO NOTE: The distance above covers the short walk between the two museums. An evening visit to the MFA is possible Wednesday to Friday, while the Gardner is open until 9pm every Thursday. If you are quick getting around the museums, you can easily progress to Route 7.

Such are the treasures contained inside these two museums that you should set aside a day for them – to spend anything less would be doing the wonderful collections a disservice.

MUSEUM OF FINE ARTS

Second only to New York's Metropolitan among American museums, the **Museum of Fine Arts ❶** (MFA; 465 Huntington Avenue; www.mfa. org; Sat–Tue 10am–5pm, Wed–Fri 10am–10pm) first opened in 1870. It moved into the present building, designed by Guy Lowell, in 1909. The I. M. Pei Wing was added in 1981 and the Foster + Partners-designed Art of Americas Wing opened in November 2010.

The highly cultured citizens of 19th-century Boston were keen collectors of amassing art and antiquities from around the world. Their bequests have resulted in the MFA not only having one of the foremost holdings outside Paris of Impressionist painting (in particular works by Monet, Pissarro, Sisley, Renoir, and Manet), but also an outstanding collection of Japanese and other Asian art. The American art collection is also one of the best in the US and those of Nubian and Egyptian artefacts are practically unrivaled too. Decorative arts include superb displays of silver, porcelain, furniture, jewellery, and musical instruments.

There is so much to see here that time-pressed visitors are well advised either to pick out just one or two collections, or take one of the (free)

guided tours that highlight curators' favourite pieces from all the collections.

Approach the MFA from the T Station, and enter at the Huntington Street entrance, outside of which Cyrus Edwin Dallin's bronze equestrian statue *Appeal to the Great Spirit* has stood since 1913.

Art of the Americas Wing

The MFA's excellent collection of American art is housed in the new four-level Art of the Americas Wing.

Among the works to look out for are portraits by John Singleton Copley, Gilbert Stuart (including the one of George Washington that was the source of the design on the dollar bill), and John Singer Sargent: his *The Daughters of Edward Darley Boit* is a particularly striking composition, and he painted the spectacular murals of scenes from Greek mythology around the **Upper Rotunda** in the centre of the MFA.

Other highlights include paintings from the mid-19th century Hudson River School and those of Edward Hopper from the 20th century. There is also a fine collection of American decorative arts, including silver made by Paul Revere.

In the glass-enclosed courtyard linking the new to the old building is the **New American Café** see ❶, an ideal place to refuel before tackling the rest of the museum. Apart from this, the MFA also offers a fine dining restaurant, Bravo, or for more casual snacks, the self-service Garden Cafeteria, with seating in the Calderwood Courtyard during the summer.

Asian art

Visitors to the MFA are frequently surprised to find it has one of the largest collections of Japanese art outside Japan, spread over two floors of **the Art of Asia, Oceania and Africa** in the museum's southwestern section. A highlight is a temple-like room displaying six massive Buddhas. Take time also to view the intricate beauty of the displayed woodblock prints, textiles, and painted silk screens.

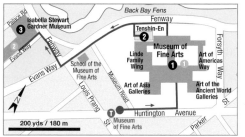

Contemporary art

Another transformation at the MFA has been the unveiling of the Linde Family Wing for Contemporary Art, located in the I. M. Pei-designed portion of the museum. This wing's seven thematically installed collections aim

Japanese-style garden Tenshin-En

to make contemporary art more accessible to visitors, jolting them with provoking questions and quirky new ideas and designs. Neon, video, sound and metallic tapestry are all part of the fascinating mix.

Egyptian treasures

For 40 years from 1905, Harvard University and the MFA collaborated on an archeological excavation in Egypt, based at the Great Pyramids at Giza. From this the museum acquired a world-famous collection of **Egyptian antiquities**, located in the Art of the Ancient World galleries. Among many Old Kingdom sculptures is a beautiful statue of King Mycerinus, who built the Third Pyramid at Giza, and his queen, dated to around 2548–2530BC. Other treasures include gilded and painted mummy masks, and some remarkably well-preserved hieroglyphic inscriptions.

The Giza expedition's director, Dr George A. Reisner, also worked in the Sudan, and brought home a dazzling collection of Nubian artefacts, the best in the world outside Khartoum. The exquisite gold jewelry, inlaid with enamel and precious stones, is particularly awe-inspiring.

Tenshin-En

Exit the MFA via its State Street Corporation Fenway Entrance flanked by *Night & Day*, two giant bronze baby heads by Antonio López García. Before moving on to the next museum, gather your thoughts in the MFA's Japanese-style walled garden, **Tenshin-En ②** (mid-April to mid-October, 10am to 4pm). Meaning the Garden of the Heart of Heaven, this tranquil space was designed by Kyoto artist Kinsaku Nakane to suggest the landscape of New England.

Renzo's vision

Much of the charm of the Isabella Stewart Gardner Museum is the result of a stipulation in Mrs Gardner's will that everything in the palazzo remain exactly as she arranged it. However, over a century into the museum's life, with annual admission numbers of over 200,000, it was becoming clear the building was straining at its seams. Award-winning Italian architect Renzo Piano was hired to design a new wing, creating a more fitting entrance to the museum, and to house such things as the café, greenhouses, education centre, and other visitor services. The museum's famous musical events also have a new home here in a 300-seat performance hall with three balcony levels surrounding a central stage. The mainly glass structure allows views of Fenway Court and is an inspired, modern complement to Gardner's unique creation.

ISABELLA STEWART GARDNER MUSEUM

Follow the Fenway around to Evans Way Park and the entrance (see fea-

Upper Rotunda   *Isabella Stewart Gardner Museum's courtyard*

ture, opposite) to the magical **Isabella Stewart Gardner Museum ❸** (www.gardnermuseum.org; Wed–Mon 11am–5pm, Thu until 9pm). Fenway Court, the Venetian-style palazzo that houses the museum, was built in 1902 by heiress Isabella Stewart (1840–1924), an eccentric New Yorker who married Jack Lowell Gardner. She scandalized Boston society by drinking beer rather than tea, and walking her pet lions in the Back Bay. Her portrait by John Singer Sargent reveals what was then considered a daring décolletage, but on seeing the notorious picture here at Fenway Court (it hangs in the Gothic Room on the third floor), you might well wonder what all the fuss was about.

The collection

The renowned art historian Bernard Berenson advised Mrs Gardner on acquisitions, but their presentation and positioning is the result of her inimitable approach. Among the eclectic collection you will see Dutch baroque and Italian Renaissance masterpieces, Titians and Rembrandts, Whistlers and Sargents, Matisses and Manets, stained glass, and textiles. As part of the museum's renovation, the Tapestry Room, which used to double up as a concert venue, has been restored to its original glory.

Even those impervious to the aesthetic qualities of this impressive collection are sure to delight in the central courtyard and museum's gardens. Mrs Gardner was also a passionate horticulturalist and gardener and many of the courtyard's elements were imported from Venice; it is ablaze with flowers and greenery throughout the year.

For refreshments head to the **Café G**, see ❷, in the new wing.

Food and drink

❶ NEW AMERICAN CAFÉ

Museum of Fine Arts, 465 Huntington Avenue; Sat–Tue 10am–4pm, Wed–Fri 10am–8pm; $$

Creative regional dishes and drinks from around the Americas form the menu of the MFA's casual restaurant and café. The hot and cold plates are prepared with seasonal, local produce.

❷ CAFÉ G

Isabella Stewart Gardner Museum, 280 Fenway; tel: 617-566-1088; Wed–Mon 11am–4pm, Thu until 8pm; $$

This well-regarded café has found an expanded home in the Renzo Piano addition to the museum; in good weather there is outdoor seating. The seasonal menu is delicious enough to throw local reviewers into fits of ecstasy, particularly over its famous bread pudding. You can eat here without paying to visit the museum.

Preparing a classic cocktail

THE SOUTH END

Few Boston neighborhoods have gone on such a roller-coaster ride of respectability and real-estate values as the South End. Today it is a magnet for artists, trendy singletons, and young families, all attracted by the area's architecture, shops, galleries, and restaurants.

DISTANCE: 2.75 miles (4.5km)
TIME: A half day
START/END: Back Bay/South End T Station
POINTS TO NOTE: Do this route in the morning, so you can have breakfast at Charlie's Sandwich Shoppe. You may wish to extend the time taken to walk the route by browsing the South End's many shops and galleries.

The South End, immediately south of Back Bay, is delineated by the Southwest Corridor, Berkeley Street, and Harrison and Massachusetts avenues. A protected historic district, little has changed since it was laid out in the mid-19th century, making the South End a delightful area to explore. For a brief period the South End was the place to live, but by the end of 19th century its wealthier residents had decamped to the more fashionable Back Bay, leaving the area largely to the working class and poor immigrants. Only in the early 1970s did the South End begin to appeal to 'urban pioneers', who saw the intrinsic value of the run-down buildings and were willing to restore them.

An impressive ethnic diversity characterizes much of the neighborhood, with scores of nationalities residing here. It is inner-city Boston's most recognizably gay area, although these days preppy young heterosexual families are more common on its streets.

CARLETON COURT PARK

Start this route at the Dartmouth Street exit of **Back Bay/South End Station**, beside Copley Place Mall. Taking up much of Carleton Street is **Carleton Court Park ❶**, which is part of the Southwest Corridor, a 52-acre (21-hectare) landscaped ribbon of park that runs for several miles southwest toward the suburb of Jamaica Plain.

BRADDOCK PARK

Walk through the park and exit left onto **Braddock Park ❷**. This small

Victorian iron railings

Playing at the Jorge Hernández Cultural Center

street is typical of the leafy residential squares that pepper the South End, all of which have a long, narrow garden, enclosed by wrought-iron railings.

At the end of Braddock Park, you could turn left on Columbus Avenue to enjoy a fine breakfast at **Charlie's Sandwich Shoppe**, see ❶.

HARRIET TUBMAN PARK

Cross Columbus Avenue to reach its sharp-angled intersection with Warren Avenue. Here you will find tiny **Harriet Tubman Park** ❸, standing in the lee of the Concord Baptist Church, and graced with two impressive statues. The park is dedicated to the 'Moses of the South,'

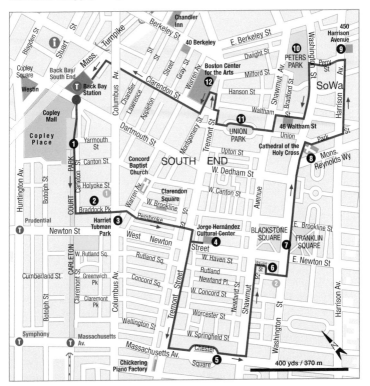

a runaway slave who organized the 'Underground Railroad.' The red-brick church was built in the 1870s, when many Baptist congregations moved to the South End.

JORGE HERNÁNDEZ CULTURAL CENTER

From the park follow tranquil Pembroke Street south to Tremont Street. Turn right and cross the road to find West Newton Street. At no. 85 the **Jorge Hernández Cultural Center** ❹ (www. iba-etc.org) is housed in a converted 19th century church. The center provides an arts space for the South End's large Hispanic community.

Return to Tremont Street and continue west toward the major junction with Massachusetts Avenue.

CHESTER SQUARE

Turn left from Tremont Street onto Massachusetts Avenue and walk southwest into **Chester Square** ❺, planned in 1850 as an oval park and once the grandest of the South End's squares. Try to imagine how the square looked then, with a fountain at the center.

Ducking left into the far more pleasant Shawmut Avenue, continue until you reach narrow **Haven Street** ❻, where you should hang a right to discover, at **no. 9**, a charming wooden house (c.1830) that is one of only two such remaining in the South End. Fac-

ing the house are the Rutland Washington Community Gardens, small allotments of which there are several in the area. You can pause for refreshments at **Flour Bakery and Café**, see ❷, on the corner of Rutland and Washington streets. If you are wondering why Washington Street is so wide, it is because it once had an elevated train line – the Washington Street 'El' – running along it.

BLACKSTONE AND FRANKLIN SQUARES

A block northeast of the Flour Bakery grassy **Blackstone and Franklin squares** ❼ lie either side of Washington Street. Planned by Charles Bulfinch as a whole oval square in 1801, it was eventually constructed in 1847 as two separate, identical spaces. The cast-iron centerpiece fountains are original.

CATHEDRAL OF THE HOLY CROSS

Further northeast along Washington Street, at no. 1400, it is impossible to miss the towering granite facade of the **Cathedral of the Holy Cross** ❽ (http://holycrossboston.com). Finished in 1875, and still one of the world's largest Gothic cathedrals, it is the seat of the Catholic archbishop in Boston. Pop inside to view the enormous interior, with seating room for 3,500, and many stained-glass windows.

Skywalk Observatory and South End cityscape

SOWA

Turn right beside the cathedral into Union Park Street, continuing to the junction with Harrison Avenue where you should turn left. You are now in the heart of hip **SoWa** (South of Washington), where warehouses have been converted to galleries, studios, loft-style apartments, restaurants, and shops.

SoWa's focal point is **no. 450 Harrison Avenue** ❾ (www.sowaartistsguild.com), which hosts 60-plus artists' studios and exhibition spaces. There are several other galleries around here too, including one in the art-lover's bookstore **Ars Libri** (500 Harrison Avenue), which specializes in out-of-print art books.

PARKS

From Harrison Avenue follow little Perry Street northwest back to Washington Street. Ahead is **Peters Park** ❿, with its striking Soul Revival mural.

Turn left and then, after the park, right into Waltham Street. At **no. 46** is another collection of artists' studios and galleries.

Where Waltham Street meets Shawmut Avenue turn left. Immediately opposite is delightful **Union Park** ⓫, created in 1851, and the best-preserved of the South End's historic squares.

BOSTON CENTER FOR THE ARTS

A few steps from Union Park's northern end is Tremont Street and the South End's highest density of restaurants. Turn right and cross the street to arrive at the **Boston Center for the Arts** ⓬ (539 Tremont Street; www.bcaonline.org), housing artists' studios, galleries, and four theaters.

Part of the complex is the unusual **Cyclorama**. Built in 1884 to house a gigantic circular painting of the Battle of Gettysburg by Paul Philippoteaux; it is no longer housed here.

From here head north up Clarendon Street and back over Columbus Avenue to find Back Bay/South End Station.

> ## Food and drink
>
> **❶ CHARLIE'S SANDWICH SHOPPE**
> 429 Columbus Avenue; tel: 617-536-7669; daily 7am–3pm; $
> The 'best breakfast in America' is promised at this touchstone of the South End, and they are not kidding. Enjoy their delicious turkey hash and poached eggs and the priceless atmosphere of a traditional diner, with hospitable staff and regular patrons to match.
>
> **❷ FLOUR BAKERY AND CAFÉ**
> 1595 Washington Street, South End; tel: 617-267-4300; www.flourbakery.com; Mon–Fri 6.30am–8pm, Sat 8am–6pm, Sun 8am–5pm; $
> The line at lunchtime nearly goes out the door for this popular café's lattes and gourmet sandwiches like lamb and curried tuna.

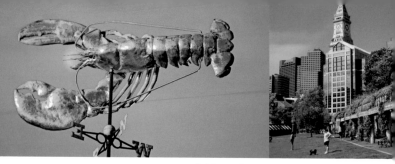

Lobster weathervane

WATERFRONT AND FORT POINT

Now that the expressway has been buried, Boston is rediscovering its Waterfront. Stroll along the HarborWalk on this route from Faneuil Hall–Quincy Market, past the New England Aquarium, to the ICA in the upcoming Fort Point district.

DISTANCE: 3 miles (5km)

TIME: A half day

START: State T Station

END: Courthouse T Station

POINTS TO NOTE: Allow for a full day if you plan to visit the Aquarium, the Children's Museum, and the ICA. The Children's Museum in particular will likely represent a fair outlay of time and energy for youngsters, so is best set aside as a separate destination, or at least one that follows lunch or a rest period. The weekend is a busy time to visit these places, so go on a weekday if possible. Entry to the Children's Museum is only $1 Friday 5–9pm, and the ICA is free Thursday from 5–9pm.

Until the second half of the 19th century Boston was the busiest port in the nation. Warehouses and counting houses occupied a dozen wharves at which clippers unloaded and loaded their cargoes. In 1878 the construction of Atlantic Avenue severed the finger-like piers from the rest of the city, a process completed with the building in the 1950s of the raised Fitzgerald Expressway. Boston turned its back on its patrimony, and the Waterfront went into seemingly terminal decline.

A reprieve came in the 1970s with the restoration of Faneuil Hall and Quincy Market. Now that the Big Dig has buried the Expressway, the Waterfront is being rediscovered thanks to development around the Fort Point Channel and the HarborWalk project.

FANEUIL HALL-QUINCY MARKET

Emerge from State T Station, cross Congress Street, and dive into the retail heaven of the **Faneuil Hall-Quincy Market ❶** complex. Quincy Market is named after mayor Josiah Quincy, who came up with the idea for the 1826-vintage marketplace. Meat and produce were sold here for 150 years before the buildings were renovated to host the souvenir stalls and boutiques found today. A tourist magnet, with frequent performances by buskers, Quincy Market consists of three long buildings. Eateries abound, including historic **Durgin Park**.

Columbus Park   *Rotunda at Quincy Market*

COLUMBUS PARK

Leave the Quincy Market carnival behind and head toward the water, crossing the strip of park that has replaced the buried expressway to arrive at **Columbus Park ❷**. A trellised walkway leads to the Waterfront. On the left stretches **Commercial Wharf**.

LONG WHARF

Immediately to the south of Columbus Park is **Long Wharf ❸**. When built in 1710 the wharf extended from near the Old State House past the towering Custom House (now a hotel) to the harbor.

Gaze out from the esplanade at the end of the wharf to East Boston and the planes taking off from Logan Airport. Setting sail from Long Wharf is still possible, either on ferries to Provincetown, the Charlestown Navy Yard, or the Harbor Islands.

NEW ENGLAND AQUARIUM

Beside Long Wharf is Central Wharf, on which stands the excellent **New England Aquarium ❹** (www.neaq.org; Apr–Oct Sun–Thu 9am–6pm, Fri–Sat 9am–7pm, Nov–Mar Mon–Fri 9am–5pm, Sat–Sun 9am–6pm). The Giant Ocean Tank makes for exciting viewing with its plethora of weird and wonderful fish, as well as tur-

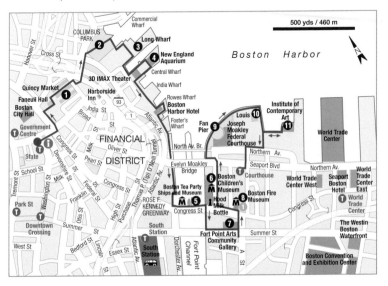

Rowes Wharf

tles and sharks. There are more than 1,000 specimens swimming around the reef to keep onlookers amused. Multiple species of penguin live in colonies around the Giant Ocean Tank and two varieties of seal are housed in the open-air Marine Mammal Center. There is also a Shark and Ray Touch Tank and whale-watching cruises for a more interactive experience.

Located just across the plaza from the Aquarium is the six-story-high **3D IMAX Theater** (daily 9.30am–10pm), which shows spectacular films of the natural world's wonders.

BOSTON TEA PARTY SHIPS AND MUSEUM

From Central Wharf continue south past India and Rowes wharves. Fort Point Channel now intersects the Waterfront.

HarborWalk

The HarborWalk (www.bostonharborwalk. com) stretches 47 miles (76km) from Chelsea Creek, north of Boston, through Charlestown, North End, Downtown, and South Boston to south of Dorchester. Designed to provide access to the restored Boston Harbor, the route hugs the coastline using established walkways as well as new paths. Nearly 39 miles (63km) of the route, also suitable to cycle, have been completed. You can download audio tours from the website to listen to as you follow the route, marked by a blue line.

This area was the bustling transfer point for many New England industries during the latter years of the 19th century.

Staying on the Downtown side of the channel, continue past the pedestrian Northern Avenue Bridge and Evelyn Moakley Bridge to the Congress Street Bridge. On a short wharf in the middle of the bridge are the **Boston Tea Party Ships and Museum** ❺ (www.bostontea-partyship.com; daily 10am–4pm Nov-March, April-Oct to 5pm), a multi-sensory adventure set back in time at the Boston Tea Party; it includes full-size replicas of the tall ships *Dartmouth* and *Eleanor*, and the restored brig *Beaver*.

Three ships laden with tea were moored at Griffins Wharf on December 16, 1773, when patriots disguised as Mohawk Indians boarded them and threw all 340 chests of their cargo into the harbor. This was the most flamboyant act of defiance against the British Parliament for its manipulation of taxes, such as that on tea, to favor British interests, and 'the spark that ignited the American Revolution.'

CHILDREN'S MUSEUM

On the eastern side of Congress Street Bridge the iconic giant **Hood Milk Bottle** stands outside the fantastic **Boston Children's Museum** ❻ (300 Congress Street; www.bostonchildrensmuseum. org; daily 10am–5pm, Fri until 9pm). Hands-on installations, including a three-story climbing sculpture and

Exhibit at the ICA   *New England Aquarium*

many games, will thrill kids of all ages. Also here is a complete two-story Japanese silk merchant's home, a gift from Kyoto, Boston's sister city.

Follow the Fort Point Channel footpath south to Summer Street, turn right and continue down to the **Fort Point Arts Community (FPAC) Gallery** ❼ building (www.fortpointarts.org).

BOSTON FIRE MUSEUM

Cross the street from the FPAC Gallery to find the stairs leading down to A Street and head northeast. Turn left at the end onto Congress Street where you will see **Sportello**, see ❶, a nice spot for Italian fare. On the corner with Farnsworth Street sits the **Boston Fire Museum** ❽ (http://bostonfiremuseum.com; Sat 11am–5pm) which occupies a firehouse dating back to 1891. Inside are gleaming antique fire engines and other apparatus.

Continue for one block and turn right down Sleeper Street for the **Made in Fort Point**; **The FPAC Store** which resides at no.70. The shop showcases pieces by the many artists and craftspeople who live and work in the area.

At the end of the street cross Seaport Boulevard to reach **The Barking Crab** between the Evelyn Moakley and Northern Avenue bridges.

INSTITUTE OF CONTEMPORARY ART

From here follow the water's edge north past the Joseph Moakley Federal Courthouse. This used to be **Fan Pier** ❾, so called because of the railway sidings that radiated out to the curved sea-wall: a small bronze model shows what it once looked like. Continue along the pier to reach the uber-chic fashion and homegoods store **Louis** ❿ (www.louisboston.com).

Beyond Louis you can't miss the **Institute of Contemporary Art** ⓫ (100 Northern Avenue; www.icaboston.org; Tue–Sun 10am–5pm, Thu until 9pm, first Friday of every month until 9pm) housed in a dramatic cantilevered structure. There are some really innovative, challenging exhibitions here and a panoramic view back to Downtown from the museum's forecourt.

Silver Line buses from the nearby Courthouse T Station will take you back to the city center.

Food and drink

❶ SPORTELLO
348 Congress Street; tel: 617-737-1234; www.sportelloboston.com; daily 11.30am–10pm, Thu–Sat to 11pm; $$
Celebrated local chef Barbara Lynch is behind this bakey café and modern interpretation of a diner: all counter seating looks onto the kitchen preparing trattoria-inspired Italian dishes. There's a groovy bar, Drink, downstairs, while Lynch's fine dining restaurant Menton (see page 118) is next door.

Boston Light on Little Brewster

HARBOR ISLANDS

*A summer trip to one or several of the 17 islands in the Boston Harbor Islands
National Recreation Area promises a blissful escape from the city to discover
nature and historic monuments that few Bostonians know about.*

DISTANCE: 7 miles (11km)

TIME: A full day

START/END: Aquarium T Station/Long Wharf

POINTS TO NOTE: The above distance is from Boston to Georges Island. Boston's Best Cruises (tel: 617 770-0040; www.bostonharborislands.org) runs ferries to the islands from Long Wharf ($20) from early May to mid-October. It takes 30 minutes to reach Georges Island from where Lovells, Peddocks, Grape, and Bumpkin islands are between 15 to 30 minutes away using the inter-island shuttle. Alternatively, go straight to Spectacle Island (15 min) from where it is possible to connect to Georges. This day-trip route is possible from mid-June to early September when the inter-island ferry operates.

Boston Harbor is dotted with 34 islands, 17 of which are protected within a state park. They are all wonderful places to relax and enjoy crowd-free hiking, fishing, swimming, and kayaking, as well as a host of other activities. Check the calendar on the website of Boston Harbor Islands (www.bostonharborislands.org) for scheduled events.

GEORGES ISLAND

From the Aquarium T Station walk the short distance west to **Long Wharf ❶**, for

Whale watching

The humpback gathering at the fertile feeding ground Stellwagen Bank, 25 miles (40km) off the Boston coast, is one of the greatest in the world. Boston Harbor Cruises (tel: 617-227-4321; www.bostonharborcruises.com) and New England Aquarium Whale Watch (tel: 617-973-5200; www.neaq.org) run whale-watching tours from Long and Central wharves respectively. The season starts in April and ends in October, peaking in June. Cruises take around three hours; commentary is provided by naturalists. Whale-watching tours also depart from Gloucester, Plymouth, and Provincetown.

Diving whale   Graves Light

the 9am ferry to Georges Island. The gateway to the other Harbor Islands, **Georges Island** ❷ is also the site of Fort Warren, built in 1833; take one of the ranger-led tours around the abandoned complex that once was a training ground for Union soldiers and a prison for Confederate captives. There is a large picnic area here (with restrooms and a snack bar), as well as magnificent views of the Boston skyline and surrounding islands.

LOVELLS ISLAND

Board the 11.25am inter-island ferry from Georges to **Lovells Island** ❸. Here you can explore the ruins of Fort Standish, search out diverse wildlife, relax on inviting beaches, and wander rocky shores upon which several ships were wrecked. Lovells is one of three islands on which camping is permitted.

SPECTACLE ISLAND

Take the 2.30pm inter-island ferry back to Georges, switching to the 3.30pm ferry for **Spectacle Island** ❹. This is the closest of the park's islands to the city and features a marina, visitor center, café, and a swimming beach. Follow part of the island's 5 miles (8km) of walking trails that lead to the top of a 157ft (48m) hill offering panoramic views. There are direct ferries from Spectacle Island to Long Wharf and back.

OTHER ISLANDS

Around a mile south of Georges lies **Peddocks Island** ❺, the third-largest harbor island, which has many walking trails, and the remains of Fort Andrews.

Grape Island ❻ has a campsite, and offers trails along which you are sure to see wildlife and birds among the wild berry trees. Camping is also allowed on **Bumpkin Island** ❼.

Only open for tours (see www.bostonharborislands. org/tour-lighthouse) **Little Brewster** ❽ is home to Boston Light, the first and oldest lighthouse in the US. The present building was constructed in 1782 after the British had blown up the original. It is the only lighthouse in the nation still manned by resident keepers.

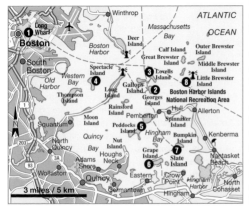

Witch House

SALEM

There is more to Salem, 16 miles (26km) north of Boston, than witches, as you will discover on this walk around one of New England's most historic towns, which is home to the exceptional Peabody Essex Museum, a treasure trove of art and culture from around the world.

DISTANCE: 3.5 miles (5.5km)
TIME: A full day
START/END: Salem Station
POINTS TO NOTE: The distance above is that of the walking route around Salem. To get to Salem (16 miles/26km north of Boston), take a train from the city's North Station (22 minutes; $7.50) on the Newburyport/Rockport Commuter Rail Line (www.mbta.com). Alternatively, from May to October ferries run from Central Wharf next to the New England Aquarium in Boston to Blaney Street Wharf in Salem (www.bostonsharborcruises.com/salem-ferry; one way/round-trip $25/45). The voyage by ferry takes 45 minutes.

Salem – the name derives from the Hebrew *shalom* (peace) – was once one of the nation's great seaports. It produced the country's first millionaires, and has the architectural and cultural heritage to prove it in its McIntire Historic District and the protected properties of the Peabody Essex Museum.

However, it does not take long to find reminders of the activities most often associated with the town – the trials and executions of 'witches.'

Just off Essex Mall on New Liberty Street is the National Park Visitor Center (www.nps.gov/sama; May–Oct daily 10am–5pm, Nov–Apr Wed–Sun 10am–4pm), where you can pick up maps

Salem's witch hysteria

In 1692, between June and September, Salem fell under a dark spell of mass hysteria, and executed 14 women and six men for witchcraft. You would be forgiven for thinking that the town is still obsessed with witches, for that sad history, portrayed in the iconic Arthur Miller play *The Crucible*, is recalled at many sites – a few historical, others kitsch. Every October the town ramps up its black-arts connection further to run a month-long celebration called Haunted Happenings (www.hauntedhappenings.org), culminating in the crowning of the king and queen of Halloween on the 31st.

Figurehead in the Peabody   Interior of Peabody Essex Museum

and leaflets, consult the park rangers, and watch an excellent 25-minute film about the county's history. Tourist information is also available at www.salem.org.

WITCH DUNGEON MUSEUM

Starting from **Salem Station**, ascend the steps at the end of the platform, cross the busy road, and walk down Washington Street, turning right onto Lynde Street after two blocks. At no. 16 is the **Witch Dungeon Museum ❶** (www.witchdungeon.com; daily Apr–Nov 10am–5pm), where you can watch a vividly staged re-enactment of a trial, adapted from a 1692 manuscript, before being guided through the tiny dank dungeons in which the accused were held.

Witch House

The nearby spooky wooden house on the corner of Essex and North streets is the **Witch House ❷** (www.salemweb.

com/witchhouse; mid-May–Nov daily 10am–5pm), where trial magistrate Jonathan Corwin cross-examined more than 200 suspected witches; the decor is authentic to the period.

MCINTIRE HISTORIC DISTRICT

Named after Samuel McIntire (1757–1811), one of the foremost American architects of his day, this historic area of Salem, roughly bounded by Federal, Flint, Broad, and Summer/North streets, showcases four centuries of architectural styles. It is possible to look inside several of the houses in the McIntire Historic District and elsewhere around town by arrangement with the Peabody Essex Museum, which manages 22 buildings around Salem.

Historic houses

Backtrack from the Witch House to Federal Street, where at no. 80 stands the McIntire-designed **Peirce-Nichols House ❸** (c.1782). The house's restored east parlor is open for tours by arrangement with the Peabody Essex Museum.

Return to Essex Street and proceed to no. 318, the Georgian-period **Ropes Mansion ❹**, which stands in a beautiful garden, and features a rare collection of Nanking por-

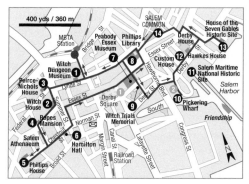

Derby House

celain and Irish glass. Across the road at no. 337 is the **Salem Athenaeum** (www.salemathenaeum.net; Tue–Wed and Fri 1–5pm, Thu 5–9pm, Sat 10am–2pm).

Turn into quaint Botts Court and walk to Chestnut Street, one of Salem's finest thoroughfares. At no. 34 is the elegant **Phillips House** ❺ (www.historicnewengland.org; June–Oct Tue–Sun 11am–5pm, Nov–May Sat–Sun 11am–5pm (last tour 4pm)) where the carriage house contains several antique cars. Retrace your steps back along Chestnut Street to no. 9, the red-brick Federalist gem **Hamilton Hall** ❻ (www.hamiltonhall.org), now used for weddings and other events.

PEABODY ESSEX MUSEUM

From the corner of Chestnut Street turn left onto Summer Street and then right at Essex Street to reach the pedestrian Essex Mall, recognizable by the red paving that matches the red bricks of the buildings. Turn right onto Central Street for **Red's Sandwich Shop**, see ❶.

Back on the Mall, reserve a decent block of time to visit the outstanding **Peabody Essex Museum** ❼ (http://pem.org; Tue–Sun 10am–5pm) where an impressive contemporary building by Moshe Safdie displays a fraction of the collection of nearly a million objects.

The museum's origins date back to 1799 and to the art and antiques amassed by Salem's seafaring merchants on their global travels. Ships'

models, figureheads, nautical instruments, charts, and maps abound. There is also a 200-year-old Chinese merchant's home transported from China and rebuilt as part of the museum; entry to this is by timed ticket, and advance reservations are advised.

PHILLIPS LIBRARY

Diagonally opposite the Peabody Essex Museum, a mini architectural park surrounds the red-brick **Phillips Library** ❽ (http://pem.org; Wed–Thu 10am–4.30pm), which has a lovely reading room. Notice the stark contrast between the massive columns of the **Andrew-Safford House** (1819; 13 Washington Square) and, behind it, the tiny features of the **Derby-Beebe Summerhouse** (1799).

WITCH TRIALS MEMORIAL

Follow the short footpath around the eastern side of the Peabody until you reach Charter Street. Here, next to the Burying Point Cemetery – resting place of witch judge John Hathorne – is the most poignant of all Salem's witch-connected sites. The **Witch Trials Memorial** ❾, dedicated by Holocaust survivor and renowned writer Elie Wiesel in 1992, is a contemplative space surrounded by 20 stone benches etched with the trial victims' names, and shaded by a clump of black locust trees – reputedly the kind from which the convicted were hanged.

Replica of the Friendship

Custom House

SALEM MARITIME NATIONAL HISTORIC SITE

From the cemetery, cross Derby Street and walk along its southern side toward **Pickering Wharf** ⑩, a touristy collection of stores and restaurants including several antiques shops. The best place to eat here is **Finz**, see ②.

Next to the wharf, the **Salem Maritime National Historic Site** ⑪ focuses on Salem's port. Stop by the **Orientation Center** to find out about ranger-guided tours of the nearby Custom House, Derby House, and Narbonne House, as well as the *Friendship*, a full-scale replica of a 1797 three-masted East India merchant ship. It is docked at Derby Wharf, one of the few wharves that remain from the 40 of Salem's heyday.

Facing the wharf is the **Custom House** ⑫ (1819), surmounted by a gilded eagle clutching in its claws arrows and a shield, which was made infamous by Nathaniel Hawthorne. Salem's most famous son worked here for three years of 'slavery,' on which he based the introduction to *The Scarlet Letter* (1850).

THE HOUSE OF THE SEVEN GABLES

Continue down Derby Street from the Custom House to reach, at no. 115, **The House of the Seven Gables** ⑬ (www.7gables.org; daily July–Oct 10am–7pm, Feb–June and Nov–Dec 10am–5pm), which inspired Nathaniel Hawthorne to write the novel of that name. The small house in which he was born in 1806 has been moved into the grounds. Guides lead you through rooms stuffed with period furniture. Take a breather in the lovely garden afterwards.

From Derby Street you could walk two blocks east to Blaney Street to catch the ferry back to Boston. Otherwise, you can return to Salem Station via **Salem Common** ⑭.

Food and drink

① RED'S SANDWICH SHOP
15 Central Street; tel: 978-745-3527; www.redssandwichshop.com; Mon–Sat 5am–3pm, Sun 6am–1pm; $
A Salem breakfast institution housed in the old London Coffee House, dating from 1698. Arrive early if you don't want to stand in line. You can also get grilled sandwiches – great for a lunchtime snack.

② FINZ
76 Wharf Street; tel: 978-744-8485; www.hipfinz.com; Sun–Thu 11.30am–10pm, Fri–Sat 11.30am–11pm; $$$
The best place to enjoy seafood overlooking Salem Harbor. Consider the excellent salmon wrap or great-value haddock sandwich.

Gloucester Harbor

CAPE ANN

Maritime history, artists' colonies, grand New England mansions, and spectacular coastal scenery are among the attractions of Cape Ann, which is an easy day's drive northeast from Boston.

DISTANCE: 40 miles (63km) from Boston to Rockport
TIME: A full day
START: Gloucester
END: Rockport
POINTS TO NOTE: Driving is the best way to get around Cape Ann; the fastest way from Boston is along Route 128, while the most scenic is along MA 127, which follows the coast beyond Salem. Both Gloucester and Rockport are accessible by train from Boston's North Station, and you can get around on Cape Ann Transportation Authority buses (www.canntran.com).

GLOUCESTER

Founded in 1623 by English fishermen, **Gloucester** ❶ is the nation's oldest seaport. Unlike Salem, its harbor is still fairly active, with many fishermen now of Portuguese or Italian descent.

If you head into Gloucester along Route 127 from the west, just over the drawbridge spanning the Annisquam

Canal you will see the **Fisherman's Monument Ⓐ**.

Cape Ann Museum

In town begin at **Cape Ann Museum Ⓑ** (27 Pleasant Street; www.capeannmuseum.org; Tue–Sat 10am–5pm, Sun 1–4pm), which displays seascapes by the American maritime painter Fitz Hugh Lane.

Walk west along Middle Street, at no. 49, is the **Sargent House Museum Ⓒ** (http://sargenthouse.org; late May–early Sept Fri–Sun noon–4pm), the home of Judith Sargent and John Murray, where rooms are arranged as they might have been in 1782 when the house was built.

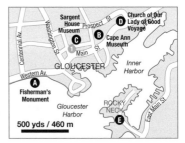

Colorful fishing floats　　　　　　*Lobster shack in Rockport*

A block south, toward the harbor, you will find several lunch options on Main Street, including **Passports**, see ①.

Further inland, on Main Street, is the attractive Portuguese **Church of Our Lady of Good Voyage ⓓ**, recognizable by its two blue cupolas.

Rocky Neck and Eastern Point

From the church, drive around the harbor to East Main Street, off of which a road leads to **Rocky Neck ⓔ** (www.rockyneck-artcolony.org): the oldest artists' colony in the US. Rudyard Kipling worked on *Captains Courageous*, about Gloucester fishermen, while staying here.

On leaving Rocky Neck, turn right onto Eastern Point Road. After about 1 mile (1.6km), take the right fork, even though it is marked 'private.' This is the exclusive enclave of Eastern Point. Open to the public is **Beauport, the Sleeper-McCann House ❷** (www.historicnewengland.org; Late May–mid-Oct Tue–Sat 10am–last tour at 4pm), built and furnished between 1907 and 1934 by Henry Davis Sleeper, a collector of American art and antiquities.

ROCKPORT

About 7 miles (11km) northeast of Gloucester is picturesque **Rockport ❸**, once a shipping center for locally cut granite. In the 1920s Rockport was discovered by artists; it remains an art colony today. A dozen galleries display works of both local and international artists on Main Street, but what attracts most tourists is **Bearskin Neck ❹**. This narrow peninsula, jutting out beyond the harbor, is packed with tiny dwellings and old fishing sheds, now converted into galleries, antiques stores, and restaurants. Enjoy magnificent views of the Atlantic from the breakwater at the end of the Neck, just before which you will pass the restaurant **My Place by the Sea**.

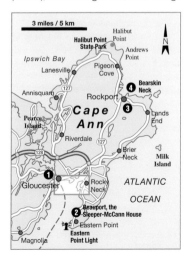

Food and drink

① PASSPORTS

110 Main Street, Gloucester; tel: 978-281-3680; Mon–Thu 11.30am–9pm, Fri–Sat 11.30am–9.30pm, Sun 8am–8pm; $
Romantically themed café; great salads, soups, and seafood.

Concord in fall

LEXINGTON AND CONCORD

*Following the 'Battle Road' between Lexington and Concord, west of Boston,
will take you past key Revolutionary sites, as well as the beautiful landscape and
classic New England locations that inspired American literary giants.*

DISTANCE: 13 miles (20.5km) from Boston to Lexington
TIME: A full day
START: National Heritage Museum, Lexington
END: Gropius House, between Concord and Lincoln
POINTS TO NOTE: In a car you can visit all the sites in this tour in a day. From Boston's Alewife T Station take bus no. 62 or 76 to Lexington center, or the hop-on, hop-off-Liberty Ride (www. tourlexington.us/liberty-ride-trolley-tours; mid-April–early May Sat–Sun, May–mid Oct daily; $28, valid 48hrs) tour covers the 7 miles (11km) between Lexington and Concord. Consider spending the night in Concord if you wish to hike the Battle Road Trail. Many sites are shut Sunday morning and November–mid-April.

LEXINGTON

To reach the start of this tour, head out of Boston on the road Route 2. Turn right at exit 57 onto the road Route 4-225. As you approach the center of Lexington there are two sites of historical interest on the left.

National Heritage Museum

A contemporary building houses the **National Heritage Museum** ❶ (33 Marrett Road; www.nationalheritagemuseum.org; Wed–Sat 10am–4.30pm), which features exhibits on the changes in America across four centuries.

Soon after is the 1635 **Munroe Tavern** ❷ (1332 Massachusetts Avenue; www.lexingtonhistory.org; daily June–Oct noon–4pm, April–May Sat–Sun 10am–4pm, hourly tours), which served as headquarters for the Redcoats.

Battle Green

Drive into the center and park. At one corner of the town common, a tiny triangular park known as **Battle Green** ❸, stands the **Minuteman Statue**, honoring the 77 patriots who faced down the British here, igniting the American Revolution of 1775. They were called Minutemen because they pledged to be ready to fight at a minute's notice.

Recreating the Battle Road skirmish on Commemorating the Patriot Day

Opposite on Bedford Street is **Buckman Tavern** ❹ (daily April–Oct 10am–4pm, tours every half-hour), a clapboard building that has been restored to its late 17th-century appearance. After the first battle of the Revolution, wounded Minutemen were brought here for medical attention.

Lexington Visitor Center (1875 Massachusetts Avenue; www.lexington chamber.org; daily Apr–Nov 9am–5pm, Dec–Mar 10am–4pm) is opposite Battle Green next to Buckman Tavern.

A short walk northeast from Battle Green is **Hancock-Clarke House** ❺ (36 Hancock Street; daily 9.30am–4pm, hourly tours). This house is where, on the night of April 18, 1771, Paul Revere awoke John Hancock and Samuel Adams to warn that the British were coming.

Before leaving Lexington you could get some refreshments at **Via Lago**, see ❶, facing Battle Green.

BATTLE ROAD

Drive out of Lexington west on Massachusetts Avenue to join the road Route 2A which shadows **Battle Road** ❻, along which the British, harried by the Minutemen, marched toward Concord. This whole area is preserved in the Minute Man National Historical Park, which has an easy 5-mile (8km) **walking trail** (see dotted line, map). Stop off at the **Minute Man Visitor Center** ❼ (www.nps.gov/mima; daily Apr–Oct 9am–5pm) to see an excellent multi-

media presentation about the start of the Revolution.

CONCORD

The handsome small town of Concord is doubly important; it was the site of the second engagement of the Revolution and also the home of renowned literati in the first half of the 19th century.

Literary homes

On the way into Concord is **The Wayside** ❽ (455 Lexington Road; www. nps.gov/mima). Louisa May Alcott and her family lived here, as did Nathaniel Hawthorne in the last years of his life. Most of the furnishings, though, date from the residence of Margaret Sidney, the author of *Five Little Peppers*.

Down the road, at No. 399, is **Orchard House** ❾ (www.lousiamayalcott. org; Nov–Mar Mon–Fri 11am–3pm, Sat 10am–4.30pm, Apr–Oct Mon–Sat 10am–4.30pm, year-round Sun 1–4.30pm), the Alcott family home from 1858 to 1877, where Louisa wrote *Little Women* and her father, Bronson, founded his school of philosophy.

Concord Museum

Where Lexington Road meets the Cambridge Turnpike is the splendid **Concord Museum** ❿ (www.concordmuseum. org; Mon–Sat 10am–4.30pm, Sun 11am–4.30pm). You can see Ralph Waldo Emerson's study, which was

Buckman Tavern

transferred pretty much in its entirety from the Emerson House across the road. The museum also has the largest collection of artefacts associated with the author Henry David Thoreau.

Monument Square

Around 0.25 mile (400m) further west is **Monument Square** (11), the heart of Concord. On the square's eastern side is the **Colonial Inn** (see page 119).

Park your car, and from the square take a stroll east along Bedford Street (Route 62) to reach **Sleepy Hollow Cemetery** (12). In an idyllic setting in the northeastern corner of the cemetery lies Authors' Ridge, the final resting place of Hawthorne, the Alcotts, Emerson, and Thoreau.

Old Manse

Return to Monument Square and drive north for about a mile (nearly 2km) on Monument Street to arrive at the **Old Manse** (13) (http://thetrustees.org; May–Oct Tue–Sun noon–5pm, mid-Mar–May, Nov–Dec Sat–Sun noon–5pm), set in immaculate grounds. From this 1770 building the Rev. William Emerson watched the battle for nearby Old North Bridge in 1775. It was later the residence of his grandson, Ralph Waldo Emerson.

Old North Bridge

From the Old Manse, stroll to the replica **Old North Bridge** (14), which spans the Concord River. On the other side stands the **Minuteman Statue**, rifle

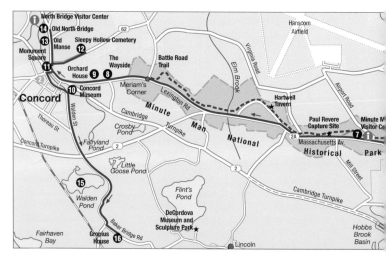

Walden Pond   *The Colonial Inn*

in one hand, ploughshare in the other. On a hill overlooking the bridge is the **North Bridge Visitor Center** (daily 9am–5pm, until 4pm in winter).

Return to the centre of Concord and Main Street to find **Main Streets Market and Café**, see ❷.

WALDEN POND

From here, travel south out of town along Walden Street, which crosses the road Route 2, for 1.5 miles (2.5km) to hit **Walden Pond** ⓯ (parking charge), which inspired Thoreau's memoir *Walden* (1854). It takes about an hour to circle the pond on foot. The best time to visit is in the fall. A cairn of stones stands alongside the site where

the writer lived in a cabin between 1845 and 1847.

GROPIUS HOUSE

Continue south from Walden Pond and, after half a mile, turn left on Baker Bridge Road to reach, at no. 68, the **Gropius House** ⓰ (www.historicnew england.org; June–mid-Oct Wed–Sun 11am–5pm, rest of year Sat–Sun only; tours on the hour). This was the first building the German architect designed on arriving in the US in 1937.

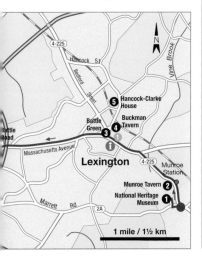

Food and drink

❶ VIA LAGO

1845 Massachusetts Avenue, Lexington; tel: 781-861-6174; www.vialagocatering. com; Mon–Sat 7am–9pm; $
Freshly made sandwiches, light meals, and other snacks are available from this convivial café.

❷ MAIN STREETS MARKET AND CAFÉ

42 Main Street, Concord; tel: 978-369-9948; www.mainstreetsmarketandcafe. com; Mon 6am–9pm, Tue, Fri, Sat 6am–11.30pm, Wed–Thu 6am–10.30pm, Sun 6am–8pm; $
Bustling self-serve hangout during the day, when it is probably best to grab a delicious cake and coffee to go and enjoy them down at Walden Pond. Live music most evenings.

PLYMOUTH

Head south of Boston to Plymouth to see the spot where 102 pilgrims landed in December 1620, a replica of the ship on which they sailed, and a living recreation of the village in which they dwelt.

DISTANCE: 40 miles (64km) from Boston to Plymouth; route: 1.5 miles (2.5km)

TIME: A full day

START/END: Plymouth Waterfront Tourist Information Center

POINTS TO NOTE: If driving, head south out of Boston along Route I-93, then the road Route 3, taking exit 6A for Plymouth center. There are direct trains to Plymouth, but the service is very limited and the station is about 2 miles (3km) from the town center. It is better to take one of the more frequent trains to Kingston, from where GATRA buses (www.gatra.org) run to the corner of Memorial Drive and Court Street in Plymouth's center. Alternatively, Plymouth and Brockton buses (www.p-b.com) run from Boston to Plymouth's bus depot, just off the road Route 3, around 2 miles (3km) southwest of Plymouth Rock.

Named after the port town in England from where the Pilgrims had sailed, Plymouth (originally spelled Plimoth) was the first permanent settlement in New England. It initially proved a benighted home for the immigrants, about half of whom died in the first winter though starvation and exposure to the elements. Only with the aid of the Native American tribes did the remaining settlers survive and begin to prosper, leading to the first Thanksgiving festival after the successful harvest of 1621.

The Waterfront Tourist Information Center (130 Water Street; www.seeplymouth.com; Apr–Nov 9am–5pm, June–Aug until 8pm) is the best place to start your exploration of Plymouth.

AROUND PILGRIM MEMORIAL STATE PARK

Begin at the **Waterfront Tourist Information Center ❶**, then proceed south along Water Street toward **Pilgrim Memorial State Park ❷**. The park's focus is **Plymouth Rock**, an underwhelming boulder that was identified in 1741 by a third-generation elder of the Plymouth Church as the rock upon

Clapboard townhouses

which the Pilgrim Fathers first stepped, in December 1620, on reaching America. Today this mythical site is protected within a classical portico.

Mayflower II
A mere stone's throw from the monument is the ***Mayflower II*** ❸ (www.plimoth.org; Mid-March–late Nov daily 9am–5pm). This boat, a replica of the original *Mayflower*, was built in England, and sailed to Plymouth in 1957. The 104ft (32m) -long vessel vividly conveys the hardships that the 102 members of the crew suffered during the original 55-day voyage.

Cole's Hill
Across the road from Plymouth Rock, climb the stone steps up **Cole's Hill** ❹ where, during their first winter on the continent, the Pilgrims buried their deceased in the dead of night. These were not marked, 'lest the Indians know how many were the graves.' Over the centuries erosion revealed some of these unmarked graves, and the remains were placed in a sarcophagus atop the hill. Near here is a fine bronze statue of **Massasoit**, the Wampanoag chief who befriended the Pilgrims, gave them food, and taught them to plant indigenous vegetables.

BESIDE THE TOWN BROOK

Return to Water Street and continue south to nearby **Brewster Gardens** ❺,

a pretty park that hugs both sides of the **Town Brook** from which the British settlers got their fresh water and herring.

Jenney Grist Mill
Cross the wooden bridge and follow the brook under two road bridges into Spring Lane and turn right onto Summer Street to arrive at **Jenney Museum** ❻ (48 Summer Street; www.jenneymuseum.org; Apr–Nov Mon–Sat 9am–5pm), located near the site of the mill established in 1636 by John Jenney.

Richard Sparrow House
At no. 42 is the oldest home in Plymouth. The **Richard Sparrow House** ❼ (www.sparrowhouse.com; Apr–Dec daily 10am–5pm), dates from 1640 and is set up so you can see how the early settlers lived.

First landfall

Despite all the fuss made over Plymouth Rock, history relates that Plymouth was not the Pilgrim Fathers' first landfall in the New World. That honor belongs to Provincetown, at the tip of Cape Cod, where a small party landed on November 21, 1620. The group explored Cape Cod by boat, until they discovered Plymouth, which offered a good harbour, high ground on which they could take defensive positions if attacked, fresh water, and fields cleared and abandoned by Native Americans.

Statue of Massasoit, the Wampanoag chief

BURIAL HILL

Follow Summer Street to Market Street and turn left into the Town Square, passing the white clapboard building (dating from 1749) that served as the Court House for Plymouth County. Opposite, also recognizable by its white wooden structure, is the **Church of the Pilgrimage** ❽. Standing between them is the stone-built **First Church of Plymouth** ❾, the longest continually active church in the US.

Burial Hill ❿ (dawn to dusk) rises up behind the First Church. It was the site of the Pilgrims' first meeting house, watchtower, and fort, whose cannons protected the harbor. There is a good view of the town and harbor from the top of the hill.

Head back downhill to Main Street, Plymouth's central shopping street, where you can turn left to find **Kiskadee Coffee Company**, see ❶.

SPOONER HOUSE

Take the second right onto North Street. At no. 27 is **Spooner House** ⓫ (June–Aug Thu–Sat 2–6pm), dating from 1749. This features 18th-century furnishings and the belongings of the Spooner family, who lived here for two centuries.

Mayflower Society House

Across the road is the impressive white-washed **Mayflower Society House** ⓬ (www.themayflowersociety.com; mid-June–early Oct daily 11am–4pm, early June and mid-Oct Sat–Sun only), dating back to 1754. There are tours of the interior, while behind the house is a library for genealogical research.

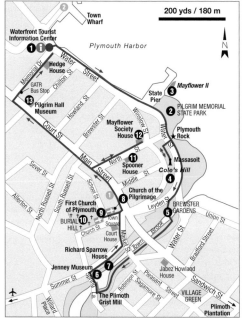

Wampanoag dress detail

English Village in the plantation

From here, retrace your steps back to Main Street which, heading northwest, becomes Court Street.

PILGRIM HALL MUSEUM

Continue north along Court Street and you will soon arrive at the **Pilgrim Hall Museum** ⑬ (www.pilgrimhall.org; Feb–Dec daily 9am–4.30pm). The museum features an extensive collection of memorabilia from the first Pilgrim families, a range of Native American artefacts, and the remains of **Sparrow Hawk**, a sailing ship that was wrecked in 1626.

TOWN WHARF

From the museum, take the next right down Memorial Drive to arrive back at the Tourist Information Center. Across the road is the **Town Wharf**, where you could end your Plymouth tour with a seafood meal at the **Lobster Hut**, see ②.

PLIMOTH PLANTATION

It is worth making a visit to **Plimoth Plantation** (137 Warren Avenue; www.plimoth.org; Apr–Nov daily 9am–5pm), where the year is always 1627. From the Town Wharf, follow Water Street southeast then Sandwich Street for about 2km (1.5 miles) to reach the correct turn-off.

In the plantation's English Village actor-guides dressed in authentic 17th-century costumes and speaking in old English dialects assume the roles of specific historical residents of the colony. The guides do not simply stand around waiting for questions, but go about their 1627 work – salting fish, shearing sheep, baking bread in clay ovens, and even playing ninepins. Even the livestock has been painstakingly 'back-bred' to approximate 17th-century barnyard beasts.

Another part of the plantation is the Wampanoag Homesite, which portrays how Native Americans lived in Massachusetts in the 1620s.

The Plimoth Plantation is also home to the intimate Plimoth Cinema, which screens foreign and independent films daily at 4.30pm and 7.00pm.

Food and drink

① KISKADEE COFFEE COMPANY

18 Main Street; tel: 508-830-1410; daily 7.30am– 5pm; $

They serve coffee here, of course, but also a big range of bagel and panini sandwiches, as well as other tempting freshly baked goods. They offer free internet which is big a plus.

② LOBSTER HUT

25 Town Wharf; tel: 508-746-2270; www.lobsterhutplymouth.com; daily 11am–9pm; $

The hut is nothing fancy, but when it comes to enjoying seafood within toe-dipping-distance of the water, then this Plymouth institution is the place to head.

Provincetown with the Pilgrim Monument behind

PROVINCETOWN

First came the Pilgrim Fathers, later whalers and fishermen, followed by artists, and, most recently, the gay and lesbian community. Now everyone heads to Provincetown, at the hooked tip of Cape Cod, to enjoy its laid-back atmosphere and fantastic national park-protected dunes and beaches.

DISTANCE: 115 miles (186km) from Boston to Provincetown by road; 57 miles (92km) by ferry

TIME: A full day

START/END: Provincetown's MacMillan Wharf

POINTS TO NOTE: The fastest way to Provincetown is by ferry. If driving, head south out of Boston along the road Route I-93, then Route 3, cross the Sagamore Bridge, then follow Route 6, which runs for 60 miles (100km), down the hooked spine of Cape Cod to Provincetown. More scenic is traveling part of the way on Route 6a, running parallel to Route 6 to the west, and passing through several of the Cape's prettiest villages, such as Sandwich and Barnstable. Provincetown is a seasonal destination; many places are closed during much of December and March and all of January and February.

Thick with craft shops, art galleries, stores selling nick-nacks and antiques, cafés, restaurants, and bars, 'P-town' is an unashamed tourist destination, but also, thanks to strict town ordinances, a beautiful-looking one. It is no surprise to find that generations of artists have been drawn to Provincetown and continue to practice here.

An hour-and-a-half ferry ride from Boston (or a two-hour drive), it is possible to make Provincetown a daytrip, although it is far better experienced on an overnight stay. Hiring a bicycle is recommended as distances from one end of Provincetown to the other are long; try Arnold's (tel: 508-487-0844), just to the left as you leave MacMillan Wharf at 329 Commercial Street, or Ptown Bikes (tel: 508-487-8735; www.ptownbikes.com) at 42 Bradford Street.

Maps and other tourist information are available at the Chamber of Commerce (http://ptownchamber.com; Jan–Mar Mon and Fri 11am–3pm, Apr–May and Nov–Dec Mon–Sat 10.30am–5pm, June–Oct daily 9am–6.30pm), on the right as you leave MacMillan Wharf. See also www.provincetown.com.

Typical architecture

FERRY FROM BOSTON

The following route assumes you will arrive in Provincetown by ferry. Running between May and October, there are several fast ferries daily (90 minutes; $93 round trip), with little to choose between the services of **Boston Harbor Cruises** (www.bostonharborcruises.com), departing from Long Wharf, near the New England Aquarium, and **Bay State Cruise Company** (www.baystatecruisecompany.com), departing from the World Trade Center on Seaport Boulevard.

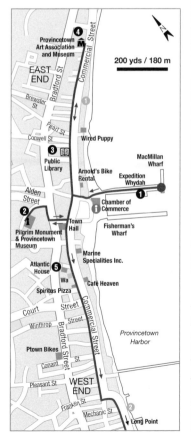

MacMillan Wharf

Ferries dock at **MacMillan Wharf**, toward the end of which you will find the **Expedition Whydah** ❶ (www.discoverpirates.com; mid-April–Oct daily 10am–5pm), a small museum documenting the remains of the pirate ship *Whydah*, which sank in 1717 off the coast of the Cape. Continue down the wharf, past the many boats offering whale watching and other ocean-going tours, to the Chamber of Commerce office for tourist information. Immediately ahead is Commercial Street, Provincetown's principal retail thoroughfare.

PILGRIM MONUMENT

Approaching Provincetown from land or sea, you cannot miss the slender granite tower rising up 252ft, 7.5in (77m) from High Pole Hill. To reach the **Pilgrim Monument and Provincetown Museum** ❷ (www.pilgrim-monument.org; daily Apr–Nov 9am–5pm), walk inland from Commercial to Bradford Street, then hike up High Poll Hill Road.

Tourist cabins

Inspired by the Torre del Mangia in Siena and completed in 1910, the monument commemorates the Pilgrims' stop in Provincetown in 1620 for six weeks before they moved on to Plymouth. To get your bearings of Provincetown's confusing geography, and for a grand 360-degree view of the Lower Cape, it is worth slogging up the tower's 116 steps and 60 ramps. The fascinating museum at the monument's base is strong on local history, and includes a section on the Arctic explorations of townsman Donald MacMillan (1874–1970).

THE EAST END

Return to Commercial Street and head left toward the **East End**. This is the artistic end of Provincetown, packed with galleries; you will find a concentration around **The Mews**, see ①. Before reaching there, pop into the **Public Library** ③ (356 Commercial Street; www.provincetownlibrary.org; Mon and Fri 10am–5pm, Tue–Thu 10am–8pm, Sat–Sun 1–5pm), surely the only library in the world to house a fully-masted half-size replica of an Indian Schooner (the *Rose Dorothea*).

Provincetown Art Association
At no. 379 you can get a caffeine boost at **Wired Puppy** (www.wiredpuppy. com), then power on to the **Provincetown Art Association and Museum** ④ (PAAM; www.paam.org; Thu–Sun noon–5pm) at no. 460. Top-class exhibitions are staged here, maintaining a tradition that started in 1899 with the founding of the Cape Cod School of Art by Charles Hawthorne.

THE WEST END

Return to the center of town and continue along Commercial Street toward the **West End**. On the way you will pass many Provincetown mainstays, including the surplus store **Marine Specialties Inc**. at no. 235, an Ali Baba's cave of sale items; the historic **Atlantic House** ⑤ (4 Masonic Place; www.ahouse.com), better known as the A-House, once home to the playwright Eugene O'Neill and now an eternally popular gay bar; **Café Heaven** at no. 207, a great place for breakfast or lunch; and, at no. 190, **Spiritus Pizza** (www.spirituspizza.com), the place where everyone heads at 1am once the town's clubs have shut.

Coastal cottages
Further down Commercial Street there are a few antiques stores, but once you have followed the road left around the Coast Guard Station the shops are replaced by guesthouses and private residences, with the sole restaurant being **Sal's Place**, see ②. The numerous weatherboard cottages surrounded by flowergardens here are a sight to behold, particularly in the crisp ocean light.

Race Point Light

CAPE COD NATIONAL SEASHORE

There are pleasant beaches either side of MacMillan Wharf, but Provincetown's best strips of sand are part of the **Cape Cod National Seashore (CCNS)**, including **Long Point** ❻, the slender sandbar that hooks back into Cape Cod Bay. You can reach here by walking across the breakwater at the far western end of Commercial Street; the uneven stones can make the crossing a challenge. Once on Long Point you can aim either right to the lighthouse at Wood End or left to the lighthouse on the tip of the sandbar – going in this direction you will pass the Provincetown nudist beach.

Along the coast

If you are on a bicycle or in a car, consider exploring more of the beaches and dunes. Heading north along the coast toward the Atlantic side of the Cape, **Herring Cove Beach** ❼ is popular with families and a fine spot to watch sunsets. Further around, and pinpointed by another lighthouse, is

Race Point Beach ❽, behind which is Provincetown's airport. You will get a fine view of the area from the observation deck above the **Province Lands Visitor Center** (www.nps.gov/caco; daily May–Oct 9am–5pm), where you can find out about ranger-led walks around the national park. Note if you bring your car or bike into the national park area there is a small charge.

If you came by ferry, head back to MacMillan Wharf to return to Boston.

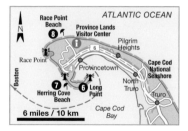

Food and drink

❶ THE MEWS

429 Commercial Street; tel: 508-487-1500; www.mews.com; daily 6–10pm; $$$

As if the classy menu and ambience – with the lower level offering dining right beside the beach – is not sufficient, The Mews also sports New England's largest selections of vodka. The food is pretty tasty too!

❷ SAL'S PLACE

99 Commercial Street; tel: 508-487-1279; May–Oct daily 5.30–10pm; $$

When other places are booked up it is often possible to squeeze in at Sal's, an authentic Italian joint in the West End with a romantic beachside terrace. The portions are huge.

DIRECTORY

Hand-picked hotels and restaurants to suit all budgets and tastes, organised by area, plus select nightlife listings, an alphabetical listing of practical information, and an overview of the best books and films to give you a flavour of the city.

Suite at The Langham

ACCOMMODATIONS

The city of Boston is well endowed with hotels, ranging from grand landmarks and opulent outposts of luxury brands, to sophisticated boutique hotels, to more subdued mid-level chains. The metropolitan area has tens of thousands of hotel rooms, of which almost half are in Boston and Cambridge. Hotel prices in Boston vary by season and most hotels tend to be in demand year-round, especially those located in Back Bay. If you plan to visit during summer, it's a good idea to book several months ahead. Another alternative is to stay in one of the many hotels in Greater or Metropolitan Boston and join the MBTA (Massachusetts Bay Transportation Authority) commuters for a 30–40-minute journey every morning and evening. These suburban hotels, most of which belong to major chains, tend to be less expensive than city-center hotels, which is not insignificant given the high cost of rooms in central Boston.

The average hotel room price in Boston tops $200 per night, and hotel tax in the Boston area is 8.45%. Deals and discounts can often be found through the individual hotels and websites, such as www.kayak.com, www.travelocity.com, www.hotels.com, www.priceline.com, www.orbitz.com, www.hotwire.com, and www.hoteltonight.com. Prices can vary greatly by season. If your travel time is flexible, call the hotel to find when their 'off-season' rates apply. During summer months, many colleges and universities in the area rent rooms in their dormitories.

All Boston hotels are required to be non-smoking.

Bed and breakfast accommodations are not thick on the ground in Boston, but those that are can be of a high standard. A couple of agencies to try are **Bed & Breakfast Agency of Boston** (tel: 617-720-3540/1-800-248-9262; www.boston-bnbagency.com) and **Bed and Breakfast Associates Bay Colony** (tel: 617-720-0522/1-888-486-6018; www.bnbboston.com). Prices typically range from $100 to $160 for a double room.

Average price for a double room for one night without breakfast:
$$$$ = more than $300
$$$ = $200–300
$$ = $100–200
$ = less than $100

Boston Common and Downtown

Ames

1 Court Street; tel: 617-979-8100; www.amesbostonhotel.com; T-stop: State; $$$

The 114 rooms at this super-hip hotel are decorated in minimalist grey and white, a contrast with the exterior decorative flourishes of this lovely 1893 building.

Room at Nine Zero

The Godfrey Hotel Boston

505 Washington St; tel: 617-804-2000; www.godfreyhotelboston.com; T-stop: Park Street; $$$

Located right in the heart of Park Street, this 242 room hotel is amazingly located and the friendly staff will make your stay all the more pleasant. The cosmopolitan rooms offer ultra-fast WiFi and streaming service from your mobile phone to the TV. The hotel's restaurant/bar, Ruka, serves Japanese/Peruvian fusion dishes and the George Howell coffee shop has a choice of beans from all around the world.

The Langham

250 Franklin Street; tel: 617-451-1900; http://boston.langhamhotels.com; T-stop: State; $$$$

Based in the historic landmark that was once the Federal Reserve Bank, this luxury hotel has rooms decorated to reflect the building's opulent history, and it has all the amenities you would expect. Its Café Fleuri offers a brasserie-style menu; it is best-known for its Saturday chocolate bar buffet and elaborate Sunday brunch.

Nine Zero

90 Tremont Street; tel: 617-772-5800; www.ninezero.com; T-stop: Park Street; $$$$

One of Boston's sleekest boutique hotels, offering high-tech, high-speed, high-touch amenities along with personalized service, custom-designed beds and down comforters. The restaurant serves some of the best steaks in town.

Ritz-Carlton, Boston Common

10 Avery Street; tel: 617-574-7100/800-241-3333; www.ritzcarlton.com; T-stop: Boylston; $$$$

Located just off the Common, this sleek luxury hotel has 193 elegant rooms – including 43 spacious suites – which feature HD flat-screen TVs, Bose radios, marble baths with separate showers, Frette linens, and pieces from a $1 million contemporary art collection. The hotel is home to the Artisan Bistro restaurant and Avery bar, and the 100,000-sq-ft (9,000-sq-meter) Sports Club/LA is accessible from hotel elevators.

The North End and Charlestown

The Boxer

107 Merrimac Street; tel: 617-624-0202; www.theboxerboston.com; T-stop: North Station or Haymarket; $$$$

This hotel occupies a restored nine-story triangular corner, or flatiron, building. It is a sophisticated boutique hotel with 80 non-smoking rooms, traditionally styled with a modern twist. The Finch restaurant serves modern American fare.

The Constitution Inn

150 Third Avenue, Charlestown; tel: 617-241-8400/1-800-495-9622; www.constitutioninn.org; T-stop: Haymarket then bus 93; $$

The Fairmont Copley Plaza Hotel

This former YMCA, located near the USS *Constitution*, offers plainly furnished non-smoking rooms, some with kitchenettes. Rates include access to a state-of-the-art health club with an indoor heated pool, sauna, and weight room.

Millennium Bostonian Hotel

26 North Street at Faneuil Hall; tel: 617-523-3600; www.millenniumhotels.com; T-stop: Haymarket; $$$$

The Millennium Bostonian is a stylish, central retreat. Rooms and suites feature contemporary decor, HD TVs, Frette linens, and some have balconies. Rooms overlooking Quincy Market can be noisy, but the location is incomparable. On-site North 26 restaurant dishes up progressive American cuisine.

Onyx Hotel

155 Portland Street; tel: 617-557-9955; www.onyxhotel.com; T-stop: Haymarket; $$$

The 112 rooms in this boutique hotel are decorated in a sophisticated palette of black, taupe, and red, and offer all the latest high-tech amenities. Their sleek Ruby Room bar hops at cocktail hour. Pet-friendly.

Residence Inn by Marriott Boston Harbor on Tudor Wharf

34–44 Charles River Avenue; tel: 617-242-9000; www.marriott.com/bostw; T-stop: Haymarket then bus 93; $$

All 168 suites at this waterfront hotel offer views of the harbor or Downtown and have fully equipped kitchens. There is a heated indoor pool, fitness room, and complimentary hot breakfast buffet. A private water taxi ($15) transports guests to Logan Airport and other harbor destinations.

Harvard

Charles Hotel

1 Bennett Street, Cambridge; tel: 617-864-1200; www.charleshotel.com; T-stop: Harvard; $$$$

The Charles Hotel offers restrained Shaker-inspired luxury, with incredible antique quilts gracing the walls, and impeccable service. All rooms are well appointed and include high-tech amenities. The Regattabar is a great jazz venue, and the Rialto restaurant is a mainstay of the city's gourmet circuit.

DoubleTree by Hilton

400 Soldiers Field Road; tel: 617-783-0090; www.doubletreehotels.com; T-stop: Harvard; $$$

On the river, next to the Harvard Business School, this is a great hotel for families. All 310 suites have two rooms, each with a telephone and TV. The living rooms contain sofa-beds, and children under 18 stay free. Breakfast is included in the room rate. Harvard Square is just a 15-minute stroll away.

Hotel Marlowe

25 Edwin H. Land Boulevard; tel: 617-868-8000; www.hotelmarlowe.com; T-stop: Lechmere; $$$$

Sheraton Commander Hotel

This eclectic and vibrant Kimpton boutique hotel near the banks of the Charles River combines high-tech amenities with family- and pet-friendly services. There are 236 guest rooms and suites, and a fitness center.

Hotel Veritas

1 Remington St, Cambridge; tel: 617-520-5000; www.thehotelveritas.com; T-stop: Harvard; $$$

Harvard's traditional crimson is banished from this intimate boutique hotel that mixes art-deco with contemporary chic. The 31 rooms are on the small side but come with lovely beds and linens and specially commissioned art on the walls.

Hyatt Regency

575 Memorial Drive; tel: 617-492-1234; www.cambridge.hyatt.com; T-stop: Central Square; $$$

The 'pyramid on the Charles,' with its striking glass atrium, is closer to MIT than to Harvard and just across the bridge from Boston University. Some of the 469 rooms offer great views of the river and Boston skyline; some also have balconies. There is an indoor lap pool with sundeck, sauna, and eucalyptus steam rooms.

Mary Prentiss Inn

6 Prentiss Street, Cambridge; tel: 617-661-2929; http://maryprentissinn.com; T-stop: Porter; $$$

This historic neoclassical Greek Revival building has 20 rooms with exposed beams, shutters, and antiques; some have wood-burning fireplaces and Jacuzzis. Rates include a full breakfast and complimentary afternoon tea. There is a lush outdoor deck, and free parking.

Sheraton Commander

16 Garden Street; tel: 617-547-4800/800-325-3535; www.sheratoncommander.com; T-stop: Harvard; $$$$

An old-fashioned but well-kept 176-room hotel near Harvard Square, off Cambridge Common. Some rooms have Boston rockers, four-poster beds, and kitchenettes.

Charles River and MIT

Courtyard Boston Cambridge

777 Memorial Drive, Cambridge; tel: 617-492-7777; www.marriott.com/hotels/travel/boscy-courtyard-boston-cambridge; T-stop: Central, then bus 47; $$

Conveniently situated on the Cambridge side of the Charles River, equidistant from Harvard and MIT, this Marriot-run hotel's river-facing rooms provide the best-value Boston skyline views.

Kendall Hotel

350 Main Street, Cambridge; tel: 617-577-1300; http://kendallhotel.com; T-stop: Kendall/MIT; $$$$

A boutique hotel in a beautifully renovated 1893 Victorian firehouse, with 73 rooms and four suites; those in the seven-story tower have Jacuzzi baths with separate showers. It is located in the heart of Kendall Square next to MIT.

Le Meridien Cambridge

20 Sidney Street, Cambridge; tel: 617-577-0200; www.starwoodhotels.com/lemeridien; T-stop: Central; $$$

As you would expect at a hotel owned by MIT (but managed by Starwood), the rooms here are big on gadgets, with Sony Playstations, dataports, and ergonomically designed furniture. The art is from the MIT collection and the DeCordova Museum in Lincoln. There is a peaceful rooftop garden, and the hotel is convenient for Central Square's restaurant and nightlife scene.

Royal Sonesta

40 Edwin Land Boulevard, Cambridge; tel: 617-806-4200; www.sonesta.com/Boston; T-stop: Lechmere; $$$

Many of the Sonesta's 400 rooms offer great views across the Charles River. There are plenty of facilities, and the hotel is close to the Science Museum, CambridgeSide Galleria, and Kendall Square. Its restaurant, Dante, serves award-winning Italian fare.

Beacon Hill

Beacon Hill Hotel and Bistro

25 Charles Street; tel: 617-723-7575; www.beaconhillhotel.com; T-stop: Charles/MGH; $$$

Just steps from Boston Common, this small hotel in a converted 1830s townhouse has 12 traditionally furnished rooms and one suite, all with flat-screen TVs and abundant amenities. It is also home to the popular Beacon Hill Bistro.

John Jeffries House

14 David G. Mugar Way; tel: 617-367-1866; www.johnjeffrieshouse.com; T-stop: Charles/MGH; $$

An old-world air hangs in this elegant, comfortable 46-room inn. Accommodation options range from studios to deluxe units for up to three people, most with kitchenettes.

The Lenox Hotel

61 Exeter Street; tel: 617-536-5300/800-225-7676; www.lenoxhotel.com; T-stop: Copley; $$$$

Understated elegance and attention to detail define this 214-room hotel, a Boston fixture since 1900. Rooms are decorated in French provincial, oriental, or Colonial decor. The corner rooms are particularly spacious, and an entire floor is dedicated to PURE allergy-friendly rooms. City Table serves New England seasonal fare, and cozy City Bar offers signature cocktails and small plates.

Liberty Hotel

215 Charles Street; tel: 617-224-4000; www.libertyhotel.com; T-stop: Charles/MGH; $$$$

The former Charles Street Jail (built in 1851) has been inventively renovated so that each of the 298 rooms integrates the building's history with a crisp, modern aesthetic. Original prison catwalks linking public spaces and magnificent soaring windows have been preserved. The pick of its restaurants is Lydia Shire's Scampo.

Liberty Hotel, based in the former Charles Street jail

The MidTown Hotel

220 Huntington Avenue; tel: 617-262-1000/800-343-1177; www.midtownhotel.com; T-stop: Symphony; $$

Conveniently located near Symphony Hall, the Christian Science complex, and the Prudential Center, this standard 159-room motel has an outdoor pool, and adjoining and connecting rooms are available.

XV Beacon

15 Beacon Street; tel: 617-670-1500; www.xvbeacon.com; T-stop: Park St; $$$$

This boutique hotel combines classic opulence with high design. All 63 rooms in the 1903 beaux arts building have gas fireplaces, 4-poster beds, and heated towel racks.

Back Bay

463 Beacon Street Guest House

463 Beacon Street; tel: 617-536-1302; www.463beacon.com; T-stop: Hynes; $$

This turn-of-the-20th-century brownstone has 19 comfortable and affordable rooms with private baths, phones, and TVs. There are also four apartments with kitchenettes, if you need more room or want a longer stay.

Boston Marriott Copley Place Hotel

110 Huntington Avenue; tel: 617-236-5800; www.marriott.com; T-stop: Prudential; $$$$

This large, reliable hotel has over 1,100 handsome rooms, a sports bar, Champions, and a laid-back lounge, Connexion.

It is linked by indoor passages to the Copley Place mall and to the Prudential Center.

Colonnade Hotel

120 Huntington Avenue; tel: 617- 424-7000; www.colonnadehotel.com; T-stop: Copley; $$$$

The Colonnade is a sleek, modern hotel. The rooms have a distinct European feel with blonde woods, chrome, and earth tones. Their rooftop pool, 11 stories above the city, is the only one in Boston.

The Eliot Hotel

370 Commonwealth Avenue; tel: 617-267-1607; www.eliothotel.com; T-stop: Hynes; $$$

Promising a 'touch of Paris in Boston' this elegant boutique option has 79 suites and 16 rooms. Also here is Clio, one of the city's finest restaurants.

The Fairmont Copley Plaza

138 St James Avenue; tel: 617-267-5300/866-540-4417; www.fairmont.com; T-stop: Copley; $$$$

With an opulent lobby and 383 European-style rooms, many with handsome period furnishings, this palatial 1912 hotel overlooking Copley Square remains *la grande dame* of Boston hotels, offering gracious service and elegant accommodations. The Fairmont Gold club level features a private lounge, and seven culturally themed suites celebrate Boston history with specially designed artwork. The new

Colonnade Hotel

elegant Oak Long Bar + Kitchen features a farm-to-table American menu.

Loews Boston

154 Berkeley Street, Back Bay; tel: 617-266 7200; www.loewshotels.com; T-stop: Arlington; $$$

Located in the former Boston Police Headquarters, this popular hotel offers 225 well-appointed rooms with Wi-Fi, multi-head showers, down-filled comforters, and other luxury amenities.

Newbury Guest House

261 Newbury Street; tel: 617-670-6000; www.newburyguesthouse.com; T-stop: Hynes; $$

Three 1880s single-family Victorian homes were renovated in the 1990s to create this elegant 32-room inn. The rooms retain some of the 19th-century decorative details. There are quieter rooms in the back. Breakfast included.

Nolan House B&B

10 G Street; tel: 617-269-1550/800-383-1550; www.nolanhouse.com; T-stop: Broadway; $

The three guest rooms in this c.1860 non-smoking Victorian home are air conditioned and comfortably furnished. There's free parking, a full breakfast, and bus service right outside the door. Rooms have shared or private baths.

The Taj Boston

15 Arlington Street; tel: 617-536-5700/1-877-482-5267; www.tajhotels.com; T-stop: Arlington; $$$

Some of the rooms and suites at this elegant hotel overlook the Public Garden. If you are lucky enough to have a real fireplace, you can ring the Fireplace Butler, who will offer you a menu of different woods to burn.

Back Bay Fens

The Beech Tree Inn

83 Longwood Avenue, Brookline; tel: 617-277-1620; www.thebeechtreeinn.com; T-stop: Longwood; $$

This B&B is bit of a hike west of the Fenway, in a turn-of-the-century Victorian home. Each of its 10 rooms is furnished with books and a fireplace. Breakfast is included, and there is a pleasant backyard patio.

Boston Hotel Buckminster

645 Beacon Street; tel: 617-236-7050/800-727-2825; www.bostonhotelbuckminster.com; T-stop: Kenmore; $$

Built in 1897, this pet-friendly hotel has 67 rooms and 49 suites. All have private baths and one to three beds and offer either a view of Kenmore Square or the Boston skyline. A Continental breakfast is included.

Hotel Commonwealth

500 Commonwealth Avenue; tel: 617-933-5000; www.hotelcommonwealth.com; T-stop: Kenmore; $$$$

In a location that is very handy for Fenway Park, this 149-room hotel is also home to the busy brasserie Eastern

The Eliot Hotel   *Churchill Suite at The Taj Boston*

Standard. Rooms feature free Wi-Fi and marble bathrooms.

The Inn at Longwood

342 Longwood Avenue; tel: 617-731-4700; www.innatlongwood.com; T-stop: Green Line D Train to Longwood; $

161 nicely furnished and fully equipped rooms in the heart of Longwood Medical Area and near Back Bay attractions. Very handy for visiting the MFA and Isabella Stewart Gardner Museum.

The South End

The Alise Boston

26 Chandler Street; tel: 617-482-3450/1-800-842-3450; www.staypineapple.com; T-stop: Back Bay/South End; $$

Some of the 56 rooms at this gay-friendly hotel are quite small, as are the baths, but they are comfortable and stylish. If you want quiet, request a room several floors up from the rowdy ground-floor sports bar.

Clarendon Square Inn

198 West Brookline Street; tel: 617-536-2229; www.clarendonsquare.com; T-stop: Back Bay/South End or Symphony; $$

Beautifully appointed, gay-friendly Victorian B&B offering the amenities of a small luxury hotel and the warmth of a small inn. Rooms have wood-burning fireplaces, dataports, and DVD players. The views of the Boston skyline from the rooftop hot tub are fantastic.

The Inn At St Botolph

99 St Botolph St; tel: 617-236-8099; www.innatstbotolph.com; T-Stop: Prudential; $$$

This contemporary hotel is found inside a unique, independent, and historic property. The Inn itself will feel more like an apartment than a hotel with spacious suites. Nespresso Coffee, David's Tea and breakfast are included.

Nolan House B&B

10 G Street; tel: 617-269-1550/800-383-1550; www.nolanhouse.com; T-stop: Broadway; $$

The three guest rooms in this c.1860 non-smoking Victorian home are air conditioned and comfortably furnished. There's free parking, a full breakfast, and bus service right outside the door. Rooms have shared or private baths.

Waterfront and Fort Point Channel

Boston Harbor Hotel

70 Rowes Wharf; tel: 617-439-7000/800-752-7077; www.bhh.com; T-stop: Aquarium; $$$$

Board the airport water shuttle at Logan and, seven minutes later, step into one of the city's premier waterside hotels. Each of the 230 rooms has either a harbor or skyline view. 18 are designed for the physically disabled. Its restaurant Meritage offers superb dining. Oenophiles should inquire about their annual wine festival.

Boston Marriott Hotel Long Wharf

296 State Street, Long Wharf; tel: 617-227-0800; www.marriott.com; T-stop: Aquarium; $$$$

Situated at the waterfront next to the Aquarium and within a minute's walk of Quincy Market. Many of the 397 rooms and 15 suites have panoramic views of the harbor; all feature internet access and a flat-screen TV.

Harborside Inn

185 State Street; tel: 617-723-7500; www.harborsideinnboston.com; T-stop: Aquarium; $$

Not actually on the water, but still in a convenient location for the Waterfront. The 116 rooms in this renovated warehouse have high ceilings, exposed brick walls, oriental rugs, and hardwood floors. Quieter rooms face away from State Street.

Intercontinental Hotel

510 Atlantic Avenue; tel: 617-747-1000/866-493-6495; www.intercontinentalboston.com; T-stop: Aquarium/South Station; $$$$

Luxury hotel well situated between Rowes Wharf, the Children's Museum, South Station, and the Financial District, and an easy subway or water-taxi ride from Logan Airport. Many of its 424 rooms and suites have Waterfront views. Its Miel 'Brasserie Provençale' restaurant serves high-quality French food throughout the day.

Seaport Boston Hotel

1 Seaport Lane; tel: 617-385-4000; www.seaportboston.com; T-stop: Seaport World Trade Center; $$$$

This Waterfront hotel has 427 state-of-the-art rooms with hand-crafted cherry furnishings, marble baths, and desks. The luxurious health club includes a 50ft (15m) heated pool and extensive exercise facilities.

Salem

Hawthorne Hotel

18 Washington Square West; tel: 978-744-4080/800-729-7829; www.hawthornehotel.com; $$$

The city's only full-service hotel is a renovated Federal-style lodging at the edge of the Green. All 93 rooms – including six suites – have 18th-century reproduction furnishings and modern amenities. There is a business center, fitness center, and complimentary Wi-Fi. Nathaniel's Restaurant serves a lively jazz brunch buffet and the Tavern has casual fare.

Cape Ann

The Addison Choate Inn

49 Broadway, Rockport; tel: 978-546-7543; www.addisonchoateinn.com; $$

A charming 1850s house that offers modern conveniences such as Wi-Fi. It has six rooms, and there is a separate cottage with two self-catering units.

Seaport Boston Hotel

Ocean House Hotel at Bass Rocks

107 Atlantic Road, Gloucester; tel: 978-283-7600/888-802-7666; www.bassrocksoceaninn.com; $$$

Three houses comprise this inn. The two-story Oceanfront and Seaside houses offer sweeping views of the sea. The main house (the Stacey House) is on the National Register of Historic Places. Bikes are available for guests. There's an outdoor pool and rooftop sundeck.

Concord

Concord's Colonial Inn

48 Monument Square; tel: 978-371-1533/800-370-9200; www.concordscolonialinn.com; $$

This historically significant inn has 56 rooms with Colonial country-style decor and modern amenities. Fifteen of the 56 rooms are in the 1716 main building (which is included on the National Register of Historic Places). The rest of the rooms are in a newer wing and cottages. The inn serves an impressive afternoon tea and weekend brunch; their spinach & artichoke dip is a great choice.

Hawthorne Inn

462 Lexington Road, Concord; tel: 978-369-5610; www.concordmass.com; $$

This delightfully decorated option for an overnight stay in Concord is located in an 1870s house opposite The Wayside. Ideal as a base for exploring the many sights in and around the town and featuring a lavish multi-course breakfast served at a communal table.

Plymouth

Whitfield House

26 North Street, Plymouth; tel: 508-747-6735; www.whitfieldhouse.com; $$

Next to the Mayflower Society House, this charming B&B dates from 1782. Fireplaces, antique furniture, and two canopy beds in two of its three bedrooms set an appropriate historical tone.

Provincetown

The Brass Key

67 Bradford Street, Provincetown; tel: 1-508-487-9005; www.brasskey.com; $$

This inland guest house is an upmarket spot, complete with a small pool and spa. Marketed as a romantic getaway spot for guests, it is pet-friendly but children and teenagers under the age of 18 are not permitted.

Provincetown Inn

1 Commerical Street, Provincetown; tel: 508-487-9500; www.provincetowninn.com; $

Provincetown is packed with guesthouses and holiday rentals. Reserve well in advance for the peak July–Aug season. Rates drop substantially out of season. This fine budget option is a motel-style resort bounded by water on three sides. It has its own pool and direct access to the beach.

RESTAURANTS

Boston Common and Downtown

Gourmet Dumpling House

52 Beach Street; tel: 617-338-6223; www.
gourmetdumpling.com; daily 11–2am; T-stop:
Chinatown; $

This phenomenally popular (and deservedly so) Chinatown place crams them in for hand-made dumplings and brilliant Chinese food; many swear by their addictively spicey Szechuan-style bubbling whole fish.

Hong Kong Eatery

79 Harrison Avenue; tel: 617-423-0838; www.
hongkongeatery.com; daily 9am–10.30pm;
T-stop: Chinatown; $

Tempting bbq pork ribs and full ducks hang in the window at this little restaurant, heavily patronized by local Chinese, which serves excellent food.

Jacob Wirth

31 Stuart Street; tel: 617-338-8586; www.
jacobwirth.com; Sun 11.30am–8pm, Mon–
Thu 11.30am–9pm, Fri–Sat 11.30am–
midnight; T-stop: Chinatown; $$

> Price guide for a three-course dinner for one, excluding beverages, tax, and tip:
> $$$$ = above $60
> $$$ = $40–60
> $$ = $20–40
> $ = below $20

This time warp in the Theater District has served wurst, sauerkraut, and beer since 1868. Also on the menu now are American standards, including nachos, burgers, BLTs, and root-beer floats.

Les Zygomates

129 South Street; tel: 617-542-5108; www.
winebar.com; Mon–Thu 11am–10pm, Fri until
11pm, Sat 5.30–11pm; T-stop: South Station;
$$$

The name roughly translates to mean 'the muscles in the face that make you smile,' and patrons here are all smiles after enjoying bistro classics and fine wine in the casual, convivial atmosphere.

North 26

Millennium Bostonian Hotel, 26 North Street;
tel: 617-557-3640; www.millenniumhotels.
com; Mon–Thu 6.30am–midnight, Fri 6.30am–
1am, Sat 7am–1am, Sun 7am–midnight;
T-stop: Government Center; $$$

Expect New England cuisine with creative flourishes: shellfish stew, chicken with sunflower pesto and farmstand ratatouille, oysters on the half-shell, specialty s'mores, and Boston cream whoopie pie.

o ya

9 East Street; tel: 617-654-9900; www.
oyarestaurantboston.com; Tue–Thu
5–9.30pm, Fri–Sat 5–10pm; T-stop: South
Station; $$$$

Union Oyster House

Inventive gourmet sushi and other Japanese-inspired dishes here will blow your tastebuds away – portions are small and designed to be paired with o ya's excellent sake selection. Start saving up for the incredible 17-course chef's tasting menu.

Sakurabana

57 Broad Street; tel: 617-542-4311; www.sakurabanaboston.com; Mon–Thu 11.30am–2.30pm, 5–9.30pm, Fri 11.30am–2.30pm, 5–10pm, Sat 5–9.30pm; T-stop: State; $$

This Japanese restaurant may have perfunctory décor, but the lines for lunch are testament to its simple, tasty food, with a few inventive twists.

South Street Diner

178 Kneeland Street; tel: 617-350-0028; www.southstreetdiner.com; daily 24 hours; T-stop: South Station; $

Classic diner fare and funky atmosphere, right down to the jukebox and all-day breakfasts. Open 24/7.

Union Oyster House

41 Union Street; tel: 617-227-2750; www.unionoysterhouse.com; Sun–Thu 11am–9.30pm, Fri–Sat 11am–10pm; T-stop: Haymarket; $$

A favorite haunt of President Kennedy, this touristy restaurant has a top-class raw bar, and serves both seafood and steaks in atmospheric rooms with creaky floors, low ceilings, and wooden booths.

The North End and Charlestown

Bacco

107 Salem Street; tel: 617-624-0454; www.bacconorthend.com; daily 5–10pm, Sat from 4pm, Sat–Sun until 11pm; T-stop: Haymarket; $$

Have a drink in the handsome first-floor bar, with French doors opening onto Salem Street, then head upstairs to an upscale Italian menu. Hearty entrées include potato gnocchi with braised Bolognese ragu and veal saltimbocca with roasted red peppers, *prosciutto di parma*, potato gratin, and a sage marsala reduction. The wine is moderately priced.

Figs

67 Main Street; tel: 617-242-2229; www.toddenglish.com; daily 11.30am–10pm, Fri-Sat until 11pm; T-stop: Community College; $$

Celebrity chef Todd English's gourmet pizzeria serves excellent thin-crust pizza grilled in wood-fired ovens and topped with a variety of epicurean toppings. The fig and prosciutto special is a perennial favorite. There's a second location at 24 Charles Street, Beacon Hill, tel: 617-742-3447.

Lucca

226 Hanover Street; tel: 617-742-9200; www.luccaboston.com; daily 5pm–1am; T-stop: Haymarket; $$$

Elegant, quiet, and dimly lit, Lucca has a sophisticated ambience that resonates in the menu – think rustic duck torta,

homemade rigatoni with wild boar, a splendid flourless chocolate cake, and an extensive wine list.

Mare Oyster Bar

3 Mechanic Street; tel: 617-723-6273; www.mareoysterbar.com; daily 4–11pm; T-stop: Haymarket; $$$

The focus at this oyster bar is on oysters and other seafood, including the likes of lobster rolls. The menu also retains some of the Italian-style dishes from the original Mare restaurant.

Nebo

520 Atlantic Ave; tel: 617-723-6326; www.neborestaurant.com; Mon–Sat 5–11pm, Wed–Sat until late; T-stop: South Station; $$

With modern decor (including sleek dark-wood tables and a marble bar), stylish Nebo attracts locals with over 20 kinds of Neapolitan-style pizzas, imported Italian meats, and rustic house-made bread. You can even choose an entirely gluten-free meal here.

Pizzeria Regina's

11 ½ Thacher St; tel: 617-227-0765; www.pizzeriaregina.com; Sun–Thu 11.30–12.30am, Fri–Sat 11.30–1am; T-Stop: Haymarket; $$

There are a few locations of this local establishment however, the North End site is by far the best. This small, simple restaurant serves the best pizza in the city. Takeaway is available.

Pomodoro

351 Hanover Street; tel: 617-367-4348; daily 5:30–11pm; T-stop: Haymarket; $$

A cozy, casual trattoria serving fresh and tasty dishes based on seasonal local ingredients. Consistent winner of food awards, and favorite among critics and locals. Come early to grab one of the eight tables. Cash only.

Taranta

210 Hanover Street; tel: 617-720-0052; www.tarantarist.com; daily 5.30–10pm; T-stop: Haymarket; $$$

An imaginative blend of southern Italian and Peruvian cuisine yields great results at this eco-friendly eatery. More traditional antipasti and pasta dishes share the menu with offerings such as pork chop with a rocoto pepper and sugarcane glaze, yucca *piatella*, and sautéed Peruvian corn, and an Atlantic salmon with herbed risotto, Peruvian asparagus, and Pisco-Sicilian blood-orange sauce.

Warren Tavern

2 Pleasant Street; tel: 617-241-8142; www.warrentavern.com; Sun–Thu 11am–10.30pm, Fri–Sat 10am–11pm; T-stop: Community College; $

Named after revolutionary hero General Warren, this historic pub has low ceilings and beams, making it a convivial spot for lunch. Burgers and chunky sandwiches are the specialty. Live music some evenings.

Salt and pepper shrimp at Russell House Tavern

Harvard

Harvest

44 Brattle Street, Cambridge; tel: 617-868-2255; http://harvestcambridge.com; Mon–Thu 11.30am–10pm, Fri–Sat until 11pm, Sun 11am–10pm; T-stop: Harvard; $$$

Chef Mary Dumont focuses on the region's freshest seasonal ingredients to prepare dishes interpreted from around the world. The atmosphere is relaxed, but has a distinct business-account feel. It offers dining in one of the few garden terraces around Harvard Square.

Russell House Tavern

14 John F. Kennedy St; tel: 617-500-3055, https://russellhousecambridge.com; daily 11–1am, Thu–Sat until 2am: T-Stop: Harvard; $$

This restaurant serves modern American dishes. The extensive menu differs from Brunch, to lunch to dinner and a separate, snack-style menu is also available. Pair the food with one of the signature crafted cocktails, local microbrews or a carefully selected wine.

The Hourly Oyster House

19 Dunster St; tel: 617-765-2342; www.thehourlycambridge.com; Mon–Fri 11am–11pm, Sat–Sun 10am–11pm; T-Stop: Harvard; $$

Seafood is the fare at this large, open and airy restaurant, with lobster and of course oysters being the main dishes. A daily 'coachman's lunch' is available Monday to Friday and American classics such as burgers are also available.

Border Café

32 Church St; tel: 617-864-6100; www.bordercafe.com; Mon–Thu 11–1am, Fri–Sat 11–2am, Sun 11am-midnight; T-Stop: Harvard; $$

A non-traditional take on Mexican meals. The menu is very heavy on Tex-Mex cuisine with some Cajun style dishes. There is a good amount of vegetarian options and margaritas are the preferred cocktail.

Charles River and MIT

Amelia's Trattoria

111 Harvard Street (Kendall Square) Cambridge; tel: 617-868-7600; Mon–Thu 11am–10.30pm, Fri 11am–11pm, Sat 5–11pm; $$

A Family-owned Italian eatery in Cambridge full of handcrafted, local, fresh foods from Paninis to pastas, salads, and meat and fish dishes. A large selection of wines from around the globe are available to accompany your meal.

Craigie on Main

853 Main Street, Cambridge; tel: 617-497-5511; www.craigieonmain.com; Tue–Sat 5.30–10pm, Sun 10.30am–2pm and 5.30–10pm; T-stop: Central Square; $$$$

Chef Tony Maw's award-winning restaurant, where quality organic and local ingredients dictate the dishes

Peach gnocchi at Dante

on the menu. Also offers a great Sunday brunch with dishes such as house smoked salmon and bluefish rillettes.

Dante

Royal Sonesta Hotel, 40 Edwin H. Land Boulevard; tel: 617-497-4200; www. restaurantdante.com; daily 2.30pm–1am; T-stop: Lechmere; $$$

Dante's outdoor patio, overlooking the Charles River from the back of the Royal Sonesta Hotel, gives it unique appeal. That the three-Michelin-starred chef Dante de Magistris also turns out excellent Mediterranean-inspired cuisine is a bonus. Dinner only.

Helmand Restaurant

143 First Street, Cambridge; tel: 617-492-4646; www.helmandrestaurant.com; Sun–Thu 5–10pm, Fri–Sat 5–11pm; T-stop: Lechmere; $$

A favorite among locals. The food is aromatic, and the flavors are exotic in an area where most of the other restaurants are pretty generic chains catering to shoppers at the nearby Cambridge-Side Galleria mall.

Beacon Hill

75 Chestnut

75 Chestnut Street; tel: 617-227-2175; www.75chestnut.com; daily 5–10pm, Sun 10.30am–2.30pm, Sept–June Sat 11.30am–3pm; T-stop: Charles/MGH; $$$

This romantic hideaway offers good American comfort food – steak sandwiches, char-grilled salmon with crispy

polenta, pasta caprese, roast chicken, filet mignon, and, for dessert, chocolate brownies with toasted marshmallow ice cream.

Beacon Hill Bistro

25 Charles Street; tel: 617-723-7575; www. beaconhillhotel.com; Mon–Fri 7–10am, 11.30am–3pm, 5.30–11pm, Sat 7.30–3pm, 5.30–11pm, Sun 7.30am–3pm, 5.30–10pm; T-stop: Charles/MGH; $$$

French food with a New England influence in a long, narrow room lined with leather banquettes and mirrors. The sophisticated atmosphere makes it ideal for intimate conversation. Weekend brunch is popular.

Lala Rokh

97 Mount Vernon Street; tel: 617-720-5511; www.lalarokh.com; Tue–Sat 5–10pm; T-stop: Charles/MGH; $$

Sophisticated Persian-inspired cuisine, with elements of Indian, Turkish, and Armenian flavors, in a romantically styled townhouse. The combination of ingredients brings the Middle Eastern food to a new level. Vegetarian-friendly.

No. 9 Park

9 Park Street; tel: 617-742-9991; www. no9park.com; Tue–Sat 5pm–midnight, Sun–Mon 5–11pm; T-stop: Park Street; $$$$

Recognized as one of Boston's top restaurants, No. 9 Park prepares European country cuisine in a Bulfinch-designed 19th-century mansion overlooking the

Scampo dining room at Liberty Hotel

Common. A simpler bar menu is also available in the bar on a first-come-first-served basis.

Paramount Café

44 Charles Street; tel: 617-720-1152; www.paramountboston.com; Mon–Thu 7am–4.30pm, 5–10pm, Fri 7am–4.30pm, 5–11pm, Sat 8am–4.30pm, 5–11pm, Sun 8am–4.30pm, 5–10pm; T-stop: Sullivan; $$

During the day this is an upscale diner with breakfast and lunch options aplenty. At night, it transforms into a candlelit café, with higher prices to match.

Scampo

Liberty Hotel, 215 Charles Street; tel: 617-536-2100; http://scampoboston.com; Sun–Wed 11.30am–2.30pm, 5.30–10pm, Thu–Sat 11.30am–2.30pm, 5.30–11pm; T-stop: Charles/MGH; $$$

Created by award-winning chef Lydia Shire, Scampo serves up contemporary Italian food with Middle Eastern influences. The lively, open space features a house-made mozzarella bar, outdoor patio, and 38-seat private dining room.

Toscano

47 Charles Street; tel: 617-723-4090; www.toscanoboston.com; daily 11.30am–10pm; T-stop: Charles/MGH; $$

Delicious Tuscan classics, including house-made pastas, slow-cooked meats, and fresh seafood, served in a warm, elegant setting of old walnut hardwood floors, painted chandeliers, and stone walls.

Back Bay

B. Good

131 Dartmouth Street; tel: 617-424-5252; www.bgood.com; Mon–Sat 11am–10pm, Sun 11am–9pm; T-stop: Back Bay; $

'Fast food' with a healthy twist. Burgers (beef, veggie, or turkey) and sandwiches are a standout, served with a variety of toppings (such as the West Side, with avocado, Aacilantro, tomato, and chipotle salsa) and oven-baked french fries or sweet-potato fries. Several salads are also on the menu.

Coppa

253 Shawmut Avenue; tel: 617-391-0902; www.coppaboston.com; Mon–Thu noon–10pm, Fri noon–11pm, Sat 5–11pm, Sun 11am–10pm; T-stop: Back Bay; $$$

An enoteca by Ken Oringer and Jamie Bissonnette, Coppa supplies delectable Italian bar snacks (meatballs, fried risotto balls with fontina, crostini with whipped ricotta), house-cured salumi, wood-fired thin-crust pizzas, roasted steaks and fish, and house-made pastas. Dishes are served as small plates.

Douzo

131 Dartmouth Street; tel: 617-859-8886; www.douzosushi.com; daily 11.30am–11.30pm; T-stop: Back Bay; $$$

Meaning 'Please come in,' Douzo is a modern, innovative Japanese restaurant and lounge specializing in fresh fish and

Roasted bone marrow at Eastern Standard

ingredients, artistic presentation, and a chic ambience and decor.

Jasper White's Summer Shack

50 Dalton Street; tel: 617-867-9955; www.summershackrestaurant.com; Apr–Oct Sun–Thu 11.30am–10pm, Fri and Sat 11.30am–11pm, Nov–Mar Mon–Fri 5–11pm; bar until 1am; T-stop: Hynes; $$

Although the word 'shack' is a bit of a stretch, few will quibble as they eat pan-roasted lobster, steamers, and fresh seafood chowder.

Sorrelina

1 Huntington Avenue; tel: 617-412-4600; www.sorellinaboston.com; Sun–Thu 5–11pm, Fri–Sat 5pm–midnight; T-stop: Arlington; $$

Serving regional Italian dishes with a contemporary twist, this sophisticated restaurant is a fancy occasion place just across from Copely Square. Their bar is a good place for a snack or cocktail.

SRV

569 Columbus Ave, Boston; tel: 617-536-9500; http://www.srvboston.com; Sun–Thu 5pm–midnight, Thu–Sat until 1am; $$$

The patio at this Italian restaurant is a wonderful place to enjoy an evening meal during the summer months. Enjoy the homemade pastas, risottos, and various small plates, all of which are full of fresh flavors.

Stephanie's on Newbury

190 Newbury Street; tel: 617-236-0990; www.stephaniesonnewbury.com; Mon–Sat 11.30am–11pm, Sun 10am–10pm; T-stop: Copley; $$

Stephanie's large outdoor patio is the place to see and be seen while dining on Newbury Street. The salads are the stars, but the rest of the menu is tasty too. In chillier weather enjoy a drink by the side of the roaring fireplace.

Uni

370 Commonwealth Avenue; tel: 617-536-7200; https://uni-boston.com/; Mon–Thu 5.30–10pm, Fri–Sat until 10.30pm; T-stop: Hynes; $$$$

Award-winning chef/owner Ken Oringer prepares exquisite Japanese dishes in this sophisticated restaurant. The food is artfully presented and every choice contains a variety of delicate flavours. Delicious, unique cocktails are available to complement the fine cuisine.

Back Bay Fens

Eastern Standard

528 Commonwealth Avenue; tel: 617-532-9100; www.easternstandardboston.com; daily 7am–2am; T-stop: Kenmore; $$$

Next to the Commonwealth Hotel, the menu at this Parisian-style bistro features everything from veal schnitzel to beef Wellington via the classic *moules et frites*. The wine list is long and well picked, and the creative cocktail menu is a labor of love. Single diners can pull up a seat at its 46ft (14m) -long bar.

Try delicate Japanese dishes and unique cocktails at Uni

The Mission Bar and Grill

724 Huntington Avenue; tel: 617-566-1244; www.themissionbar.com; Mon–Fri 11am–midnight, Sat–Sun 9am–midnight; T-stop: Brigham Circle; $$

The mission of this 'gastropub' seems to be beer, with a respectable list of bottled ales and on-tap brews. They also get the food right. French fries are made with sweet potatoes, and salads are garnished with homemade croutons, not drowned in oil.

Petit Robert Bistro

480 Columbus Ave; tel: 617-867-0600; www.petitrobertbistro.com; daily 11am–10pm; T-stop: Kenmore; $$

Simple French food without any fuss or extortionate prices. Chef Jacky Robert's goal is to create a bistro where diners can eat for under $20. Ingredients from the best purveyors create upmarket steak frites, lobster bouillabaisse, and croque monsieur. There is a second branch in the South End at 480 Columbus Avenue (tel: 617-867-0600).

The South End

The Butcher Shop

552 Tremont Street; tel: 617-423-4800; http://thebutchershopboston.com; Mon noon–11pm, Tue–Fri noon–midnight, Sat 11am–midnight, Sun 11am–11pm; T-stop: Back Bay; $$$

One of Boston's top chefs, Barbara Lynch, runs this small wine bar and charcuterie. Stop in for a generous pour of Pinot Noir with a small plate of antipasti, before a performance at the Boston Center for the Arts opposite.

Delux Café

100 Chandler Street; tel: 617-338-5258; Mon–Sat 5pm–1am; T-stop: Back Bay; $$

The quirky decor of old Elvis records on the walls and Cartoon Network on the television screens make Delux a magnet for hipsters. You cannot go wrong with their famous quesadillas or one of their comfort-food specials.

The Franklin Café

278 Shawmut Avenue; tel: 617-350-0010; www.franklincafe.com; Mon–Sun 5pm–2am; T-stop: Back Bay; $$

Delicious bistro-style dishes served in a romantic, darkly lit small space, tucked away on sleepy Shawmut Avenue. Try the seasonal sides, classic cocktails, and daily gourmet specials.

Myers+Chang

1145 Washington Avenue; tel: 617-542-5200; www.myersandchang.com; Sun–Thu 11.30am–10pm, Fri–Sat 11.30am–11pm; T-stop: Back Bay; $$$

Engaging, youthful Asian restaurant with a menu of dishes designed for sharing – their hakka eggplant is the best, while their tiger's tears, Thai-style steak is addictively spicy.

Waterfront and Fort Point Channel

The Barking Crab

Fort Point Landing, 88 Sleeper Street; tel:

617-426-2722; www.barkingcrab.com; Sun–Thu 11.30am–9pm, Fri–Sat 11.30am–10pm; T-stop: South Station; $$

A red-and-yellow tent covers shared bench tables at this casual shack-like place serving mainly seafood. It can get very crowded on summer evenings. The bar is open one hour later than the restaurant.

Durgin Park

340 North Market, Faneuil Hall; tel: 617-227-2038; daily 11.30am–9pm, Thu–Sat until 10pm; T-stop: State Street; $$

Opened in 1827, Durgin Park still retains the same pressed-tin ceilings and mosaic-tile floor, as well as the same Yankee-style cooking (think shepherd's pie and homemade fish cakes), all of which is served at communal tables in huge portions.

James Hook & Co

440 Atlantic Ave, Boston; tel: 617-423-5501; www.jameshooklobster.com; Mon–Thu 10am–5pm, Fri until 6pm, Sat 10am–5pm, and Sun 10am–4pm; $$

This waterfront shack specializes in lobster. The creamy lobster roll is the signature choice but boiled lobster, chowder, and bisque are all available as well other as other shell fish and fresh fish dishes.

Menton

354 Congress Street; tel: 617-737-0099; www.mentonboston.com; Sun–Mon 5.30–9pm, Tue–Fri 5.30–10pm; T-stop: Courthouse; $$$$

Named after a small French village on the border with Italy, this is Barbara Lynch's high-end affair serving either two four-course prix-fixe menus or the chef's seven course tasting menu: an elaborate affair that lasts all evening.

Meritage

Boston Harbor Hotel, 70 Rowes Wharf; tel: 617-439-3995; www.meritagetherestaurant.com; Tue–Sat 6–10pm; T-stop: Aquarium; $$$$

Each New American dish is available in a small or large portion and is linked to one of six wine categories. Thus diners know that pan-seared Diver scallops are best with a full-bodied white wine, and a spicy/earthy red is best for the cocoa-rubbed roast Kobe beef flank steak. Award-winning, 15,000-bottle cellar.

No-Name

15 Fish Pier (just off Northern Avenue); tel: 617-338-7539; http://nonamerestaurant.com; Mon–Sat 11am–10pm, Sun 11am–9pm; T-stop: World Trade Center; $

The antithesis of a tourist trap, No-Name serves no-frills seafood for reasonable prices in a large dining room simply decorated with blown-up photos of Boston's past. Preparations are simple, but the chowder has a reputation.

Temazcal Tequila Cantina

250 Northern Avenue; tel: 617-439-3502; www.temazcalcantina.com; daily 11am–2am; T-stop: World Trade Center; $$

This upscale Liberty Wharf cantina offers a lively atmosphere, menus on iPads, and 300 types of tequila. Go for the lobster guacamole, bean dip, margaritas, and view.

Cape Ann

My Place by the Sea

68 Bearskin Neck, Rockport; tel: 978-546-9667; www.myplacebythesea.com; daily May–early Dec 11.30am–9pm; $$

Fantastic views are guaranteed at this adorable, friendly place serving imaginative modern American cuisine. Good value for lunch, pricier for dinner, when reservations are advised.

Lexington

Sanyo

25 Depot Square; tel: 781-861-6030; Sun–Thu 11.30am–9.15pm, Fri–Sat 11.30am–10.15pm; $

Lexington has a large Chinese population; the fact that many of them frequent this restaurant proves how good the food is. The dim sum and lunch buffet are very popular.

Concord

Colonial Inn

48 Monument Square; tel: 978-369-9200; www.concordscolonialinn.com; daily 7am–9pm; $$

Dating back to 1716, this is as traditional as it gets in Concord, although all but 15 of the hotel's 60 rooms are in a modern brick annex. Meals are available throughout the day, but book at least 24 hours in advance for their formal high tea ($25) served twice a month on Sat and Sun 3–5pm.

Plymouth

Sam Diego's

51 Main Street; tel: 508-747-0048; www.samdiegos.com; daily 11.30am–midnight; $$

Enjoy tasty Mexican and southwestern cuisine on the terrace of this lively restaurant (housed in a former fire station), and watch the passing parade on Main Street. The bar stays open until 1am.

Provincetown

Red Inn

15 Commercial Street; tel: 508-487-7334; www.theredinn.com; May–Oct daily 5.30pm–late, Thu–Sat 11am–2.30pm, Nov–Apr Sat–Sun dinner only; $$$

One of the most pleasant places to dine in Provincetown is this elegant West End inn with beautiful gardens and a prime beachside position. The cuisine is modern American, and portions are generous. There is also accommodation here, if you decide to stay over.

Ross's Grill

Whaler's Wharf, 237 Commercial Street; tel: 508-487-8878; www.rossgrilptown.com; daily 11.30am–9.30pm $$$

Intimate and friendly, Ross's is the epitome of relaxed fine dining, with excellent bistro-style dishes such as steak frites and crispy Tuscan cod. There is also a wide selection of wines by the glass.

Industrial-chic Alibi

NIGHTLIFE

For dance clubs you will typically pay an entrance fee of between $10 and $25, depending on the night and the DJ playing. Bars, pubs, and lounges typically open around 4 or 5pm. By law they all have to stop serving alcohol at 2am (1am Sunday to Wednesday in Cambridge). Many places also enforce a dress code prohibiting sportswear, sneakers, and baseball caps. Check websites or call for details before heading out.

Among the top US comedians to have kick-started their careers in Boston are Denis Leary and Conan O'Brien. A couple of long-running places that put on regular shows are ImprovBoston (40 Prospect Street, Cambridge; tel: 617-576-1253; www.improvboston.com; Tue–Sun shows from 6pm, check for details; T-stop: Central) and Improv Asylum (216 Hanover St; tel: 617-263-6887; T-stop: Haymarket).

Bars, pubs, and lounges

21st Amendment
150 Bowdoin Street; tel: 617-227-7100; www.21stboston.com; daily; T-stop: Park Street
The 21st Amendment repealed Prohibition, and the lawyers, law students, legislators, and Beacon Hill locals congregating in this cozy dark pub with pews still enjoy that right.

49 Social
49 Temple Place; tel: 617-338-9600; www.49socialboston.com; open Tue–Sun; T-stop: Park Street/Downtown Crossing
A Stylish restaurant and bar that buzzes when young professionals stop by after work to enjoy a well-crafted cocktail and elegant nibbles, such as truffle mac and cheese, olives, and humus and seasoned pita chips.

Alibi
Liberty Hotel, 215 Charles Street; tel: 617-224-4000; www.libertyhotel.com; daily; T-stop: Charles/MGH
Housed in a former jail, this lounge bar fittingly serves drinks in the clink's former drunk tank with blown-up mugshots of Frank Sinatra and Lindsay Lohan leering at patrons, and a cocktail menu listing drinks like 'Doing Thyme.'

The Beehive
541 Tremont Street; tel: 617-423-0069; www.beehiveboston.com; daily; T-stop: Back Bay
Lounge bar and restaurant with inventive interior design, stylish crowd, velvet ropes, and a long line on weekends, when there's often live jazz.

Bell in Hand
45 Union Street; tel: 617-227-2098; www.bellinhand.com; daily; T-stop: Haymarket

With a prime corner location, this self-proclaimed 'oldest tavern in America' (established in 1795) is a great people watching spot. They have their own beer and a full menu of traditional bar food.

Doyle's

3484 Washington Street, Jamaica Plain; tel: 617-524-2345

An old school Irish pub which sells the largest selection of draft beer in New England. This relaxed, casual drinking spot also serves great pub classics such as garlic bread, fish and chips, and pies. For the best experience sit in the front room to enjoy the fine, informal dining.

Green Street Grill

280 Green St; tel: 617-876-1655; daily 4pm–2am; T-Stop: Central Square

The long, narrow bar gets incredibly crowded however, the wait will give you time to decide from the exhaustive cocktail list, all of which are made to perfection.

Grendel's Den

89 Winthrop Street, Cambridge; tel: 617-491-1160; www.grendelsden.com; daily; T-stop: Harvard

Unpretentious student hangout that gained notoriety in 1982 when it won an historic court case enabling them to use their liquor license within 10 feet of a church.

jm Curley

21 Temple Place; tel: 617-338-5333, daily from 11.30am–2am; T-Stop: Downtown Crossing

This restaurant and bar specializes in innovative American comfort food. The industrial-style red brick interior creates a warm, cozy atmosphere to sample selections from the cocktail and beer menus.

J.J. Foley's Cafe

117 East Berkeley Street; tel: 617-728-9101; www.jjfoleyscafe.com; daily; T-stop: Arlington

One of a few family-run old-school taverns surviving the South End gentrification wave. In business since 1909, including a Prohibition-era stint as a suspiciously popular shoe store, Foley's is favored by off-duty cops, newspapermen, and nearby factory workers for cheap pints and simple grub.

Middlesex

315 Massachusetts Avenue, Cambridge; tel: 617-868-6739; www.middlesexlounge.com; daily; T-stop: Central

At around 10pm the low, sleek furniture is rolled to the edges of the room, and the space becomes a dance floor packed with a hip, cosmopolitan crowd. Go before 11pm to skip the legendary line.

Sevens Ale House

77 Charles Street; tel: 617-523-9074; daily; T-stop: Charles/MGH

Refreshingly down to earth for ritzy

Beacon Hill, this small rustic pub gets pretty rowdy on game nights. A game of darts can become a dangerous sport on packed weekend evenings.

State Park
One Kendall Square Building; tel: 617-848-4355; daily 11–1am, Thu–Sat until 2am; T-Stop: Kendall Square
Enjoy the indoor shuffleboard table and jukebox at this tiny, but beloved bar. Sample the signature cocktail or stick to a refreshing craft beer or chilled glass of white wine.

Live music

Berklee Performance Centre
136 Massachusetts Avenue; tel: 617-747-2261; www.berkleebpc.com; T-stop: Hynes
Flagship performance space of the prestigious college of music with a highly regarded jazz program that attracts students from around the globe. Past alumni include Quincy Jones, Melissa Etheridge, Donald Fagen, and Branford Marsalis.

Club Passim
47 Palmer Street; tel: 617-492-7679; www.clubpassim.org; T-stop: Harvard
The US's oldest folk club, Passim hosts a variety of local and national artists, focusing on folk, world, and bluegrass.

House of Blues
15 Lansdowne Street; tel: 1-888-693-2583; www.houseofblues.com/venues/clubvenues/boston; daily; T-stop: Kenmore
Mid-sized rock concert venue that's one of the choice venues for chart-topping acts from the US and abroad.

The Middle East Club
472–480 Massachusetts Avenue, Cambridge; tel: 617-864-3278; www.mideastclub.com; T-stop: Central
A variety of acts play in this complex's various rooms, where the walls are adorned with local artists' work.

Paradise Rock Club
967–969 Commonwealth Avenue; tel: 617-562-8800; www.thedise.com; daily 6pm–2am; T-stop Pleasant Street
Boston's top venue for established and up-and-coming rock and alt pop music talents. For over 25 years it has hosted everyone from U2 to Bloc Party.

Regattabar
Charles Hotel, 1 Bennett Street, Cambridge; tel: 617-661-5000; www.regattabarjazz.com; T-stop: Harvard
Fashionable bar featuring well-known jazz and R&B acts in a sophisticated interior. Bookings recommended.

Sonia Live Music Venue
10 Brookline Street, Cambridge; tel: 617-864-3278; www.mideastoffers.com/sonia; daily; T-stop: Central
One of the best places in greater Boston to catch live music, in a relaxed, friendly

atmosphere. Last-minute tickets can be bought at the door with cash only.

Toad

1912 Massachusetts Avenue, Cambridge; tel: 617-497-4950; www.toadcambridge. com; Mon–Wed 5pm–1am, Thu–Sat 5pm–2am, Sun 6pm–1am; T-stop: Porter Square

Bands perform live every night at this cozy neighborhood bar (room for just 62 customers) with no cover charge. Pearl Jam have done impromptu gigs here when they are in town.

Wally's Café

427 Massachusetts Avenue; tel: 617-424-1408; www.wallyscafe.com; daily; T-stop; Massachusetts Avenue

Hole-in-the-wall bar with jamming locals performing nightly. Named after founder Joseph L. Walcott, who opened the original bar across the street in 1947.

Gay scene

The Alley

14 Pi Alley; tel: 617-263-1449; www. thealleybar.com; daily; T-stop: Park Street

Flying the flag for the Downtown gay community, this casual, friendly pub is the home of the annual Bearapalooza for the hirsute and their admirers.

Club Café

209 Columbus Avenue; tel: 617-536-0966; www.clubcafe.com; daily; T-stop: Arlington

Popular and large complex, with a dance space and video lounge to the rear and quieter bar and restaurant at the front.

Jacque's Cabaret

79 Broadway, Boston; tel: 617-426-8902; www.jacques-cabaret.com; daily 11am–midnight

It is home to some of the wildest drag shows in town. Seven days a week at Jacque's Cabaret, you can see the most glamorous showgirls from New England and beyond.

Dance clubs

Good Life

28 Kingston St; tel: 617-451-2622; Thu–Sat open until 2am; www.goodlifebar.com; T-Stop: Downtown Crossing

This compact club has two dance floors and rotates the music from hip-hop, dub-step, and electro, sometimes throwing in a few songs from the top-40 hits.

Icon

100 Warrenton St, Boston; www. iconnightclub.com; Thu–Sat 10.30pm–2am

This high-energy nightclub also has an exclusive lounge area. It is a popular last stop on Friday and Saturday nights.

Royale

279 Tremont Street; tel: 617-338-7699; http://royaleboston.com; Fri–Sun; T-stop: Boylston

One of Boston's largest clubs, with seven bars, balconies, and a huge dance floor that also hosts live performances.

A–Z

A

Admission charges

Go Boston Card: tel: 1-800-887-9103; www.smartdestinations.com. This one, two, three, five- or seven-day visitor pass offers admission to over 53 attractions and tours in and around Boston, including several popular sightseeing tours and museums. Cards can be bought online or at the Bostix booths at Faneuil Hall and Copley Square, and the Boston Common and Prudential Center visitor information centers. There is also another card – 'Build Your Own Boston' where you can choose the places you want to visit and put the pass onto your mobile, see website for more details.

Boston CityPass: tel: 1-888-330-5008; www.citypass.com. This gives admission to four sites (Prudential Center Skywalk, Museum of Science, New England Aquarium, and Harvard Museum of Natural History or The Old State House), as well as discounts at several other attractions and restaurants ($59 adults; $47 youths). It is good for nine consecutive days, and is sold online and at all the above locations.

BosTix Ticket Booth: Faneuil Hall (near the West End Entrance of Quincy Market) and Copley Square (corner of Boylston and Dartmouth streets); tel: 262-8632, ext. 229; www.bostix.org. Tickets and information for over 100 entertainment and cultural attractions. Day-of, half-price theater tickets are sold. Tue–Sat 10am–6pm, Sun 11am–4pm. Cash and credit cards accepted.

BostonUSA: www.bostonusa.com. Search this website for dozens of deals on attractions, restaurants, and accommodation around Boston. Discounts change seasonally.

Age restrictions

You must be at least 16 to drive in Massachusetts, even if you hold a valid license from another state, and at least 16 and a half to obtain a Massachusetts driver's license. The legal drinking age in Massachusetts is 21. The legal age of consent is 16. You must be 21 to rent a car; some companies require you to be 25.

B

Business hours

Most **offices** are open Monday to Friday 9am to 5pm. Federal and local government offices are usually open weekdays 8.30am to 4.30pm. **Banks** are open weekdays 9am to 4pm. Some are also open on Thursday until 5pm and Saturday 9am to noon.

Children's Museum on Congress Street

Most stores open Mon–Sat 9am–7pm, and shopping malls generally stay open until 9pm. On Sunday opening hours are typically noon–5pm or 6pm. Many smaller, independently owned shops and Downtown businesses are closed on Sunday.

C

Children

There are loads of museums to explore, shops to visit, parks to explore and activities geared specially to children. Stop in at the Visitor Information Center near the Park Street MBTA station for a variety of pamphlets and ideas on the best way to see the city with children.

Child care

Many hotels offer child-care services, which charge by the hour. Ask at the front desk.

Parents in a Pinch, Inc.: 45 Bartlett Crescent, Brookline, tel: 739-5437/800-688-4697, www.parentsinapinch.com, offers in-room hotel care for children of all ages, with a minimum stay of four hours. Prices can vary so make sure to check their website for updated details.

Child-friendly tours

Boston by Little Feet: tel: 367-2345, www.bostonbyfoot.com. Geared for ages 6–12, the hour-long tour stops at 10 sites along the Freedom Trail. Meets at the Samuel Adams statue on Congress Street. Tour times: May–Oct Fri–Sat 10am, Sun 2pm, Apr call for times. The cost is $10 (online), $12 cash. Meet 10 minutes before the tour's start time at the Samuel Adams statue in front of Faneuil Hall. No reservations are necessary, and tours are offered rain or shine.

Climate

Boston has four distinct seasons. The first snow generally falls in November and continues intermittently through March (however don't be surprised to see some snow in the early parts of April). Spring, which can be fleeting, starts in April, and is characterized by crisp, clear days and chilly evenings. June to September can be very hot and humid, although most of the summer is pleasant due to the ocean breeze. Fall is glorious, and the famous New England multicolored foliage peaks in mid-October as the temperature starts to plummet.

For daily weather updates check online at www.accuweather.com.

Crime and safety

Boston is one of the safest cities in the US, but visitors should always be vigilant. Areas where crime is a problem, such as Dorchester, Mattapan, and Roxbury, offer few tourist attractions, and are on the fringes of the city. One central area to avoid, especially

Massachusetts General Hospital

at night, is south of Washington Street and west of Massachusetts Avenue. Avoid the Fenway Victory Gardens in Back Bay Fens, as violent attacks have been reported here.

Customs regulations

Anyone over the age of 21 may bring 200 cigarettes, 50 cigars, or 4.4lbs (2kg) of tobacco, one liter of alcohol, and a maximum of $200 worth of duty-free gifts. Importing meat products, seeds, plants, or fruits is illegal, as are narcotics. The US permits you to take out anything you wish, but consult with the authorities of your destination country to learn of its customs regulations on entry.

D

Disabled travelers

Boston caters well to the disabled traveler, with accessible bathrooms and ramps on public buildings, curbsides, and at most attractions. However, it is also an old city with Colonial buildings and cobblestone sidewalks, so despite best efforts it is not always perfect. Check the Massachusetts Bay Transit Authority's website (www.mbta.com) for public transport access information for disabled travelers, including details of its The Ride service for door-to-door paratransit. For more information call 1-800-533-6282/617-222-5123, Mon–Fri 6.30am–8pm, Sat and Sun 7.30am–6pm. Boston's Commission for Persons with Disabilities can be reached on tel: 617-635-3682 or via www.cityofboston.gov/disability.

E

Electricity

The US uses 110–120V, 60-cycle AC voltage (as opposed to the 220–240V, 50-cycle of Europe). Laptops and many travel appliances are dual voltage and will work, but check first. An adapter will be needed for US sockets.

Embassies and consulates

Most embassies are based in Washington, D.C., but many countries have consulates in Boston. A complete list can be found at www.state.gov.
Canada: 3 Copley Place, Suite 400; tel: 617-262-247-5100; http://international.gc.ca
Ireland: 535 Boylston Street; tel: 617-267-9330; www.dfa.ie/irish-consulate/boston
Israel: 20 Park Plaza; tel: 617-535-0201; embassies.gov.il/boston
United Kingdom: One Broadway, Cambridge; tel: 617-245-4500; www.gov.uk/government/world/organisations/british-consulate-general-boston

Emergency numbers

To contact ambulance, Fire, or Police: tel: 911.

The strong arm of the law

H

Health and medical care

Foreign visitors needing medical attention can face stiff bills for one night in a hospital in a semi-private room. It is strongly advised to arrange medical insurance before leaving home.

Emergency dental care

Tufts Dental School, 1 Kneeland Street; tel: 617-636-6828; https://dental.tufts.edu; Mon–Fri 9–10.30am, 1–2.30pm. Emergency walk-in clinic with limited admissions.

Hospitals

Brigham & Women's Hospital, 75 Francis Street; tel: 617-732-5500; www.brighamandwomens.org.
Mount Auburn Hospital, 330 Mount Auburn Street; tel: 617-492-3500; www.mountauburnhospital.org.
Massachusetts General Hospital, 55 Fruit Street; tel: 617-726-2000; www.massgeneral.org.
Tufts Medical Center, 800 Washington Street; tel: 617-636-5000; www.tuftsmedicalcenter.org.
Boston Children's Hospital, 300 Longwood Ave; tel: 617-355-6000; www.childrenshospital.org.

Medical hotlines

Beth Israel Deaconess Hospital, tel: 617-667-7000; www.bidmc.org.

Massachusetts Eye and Ear Infirmary, tel: 617-523-7900; www.masseyeandear.org.
Aids hotline, tel: 1-800-235-2331; Mon–Thu 9am–8pm, Fri 9am–5pm; www.aac.org.

Pharmacies

Several branches of CVS (www.cvs.com) are open 24 hours, including:
CVS Pharmacy, 587 Boylston Street; tel: 617-437-8414.
CVS Pharmacy, 36 White Street, Cambridge; tel: 617-876-5519.

I

Internet

Wireless internet access is common in cafés and many student-type hangouts. Many places charge a fee for increments of an hour to 24 hours, but you can also find free hotspots (www.openwifispots.com) throughout the city.
Boston Public Library, 700 Boylston Street; tel: 617-536-5400; www.bpl.org; Mon–Thu 9am–9pm, Fri–Sat 9am–5pm. Free wireless connections to the Library's internet service in all 25 branches, with direct plug-in ports available in Bates Hall in the Central Library.
Cambridge Public Library, 449 Broadway, Cambridge; tel: 617-349-4041; www.cambridgema.gov; Mon–Thu 9am–9pm, Fri–Sat 9am–5pm. Free wireless access in all the branches, with a few internet computer stations available on a first-come-first-served basis

and allowed one 60-minute session per day. Users are allowed up to 10 pages of free printing per day.

L

Legal matters

In the unfortunate event you are arrested, you are legally allowed to remain silent, and are entitled to free legal representation, provided by the state, if you cannot afford it yourself. You are also entitled to a single phone call. If you do not have family, friends, or a lawyer that can be of assistance, call your embassy or consulate. The legal drinking age in Massachusetts is 21, and driving under the influence is a serious offense that will result in stiff fines and jail time.

LGBTQ travelers

Massachusetts is famous as the first US state to legalize same-sex marriage. In general Boston is a very integrated city, so you will find gays and straights mingling in many city neighborhoods. The South End has the highest concentration of gay bars and is also the home of the annual Boston Pride parade (www.bostonpride. org) that culminates in a huge carnival. Somerville and Jamaica Plain are popular areas for lesbians to hang out.

The **Greater Boston Business Council** (www.gbbc.org) is the city's gay chamber of commerce, with information on businesses owned, operated, or supported by the local gay community.

Bay Windows (www.baywindows. com) is a newspaper covering Boston news, gay culture, and nightlife, while *The Rainbow Times* (www.therainbow timesmass.com) has a wider New England focus.

Lost property

Most establishments operate their own lost-and-found department, but if you lose something in a public area, go to the local police station to see if it has been handed in.

Lost or stolen credit cards
AMEX: tel: 1-800-992-3404
Diners Club/Carte Blanche: tel: 1-800-234-6377
MasterCard: tel: 1-800-622-7747
Visa: tel: 1-800-847-2911

M

Maps

Rubel BikeMaps (www.bikemaps.com) produces great cycling maps for routes in and around Boston.

Media

Newspapers: The city's main daily newspapers are the broadsheet *Boston Globe* (www.boston.com) and the tabloid *Boston Herald* (www.bostonherald. com). The *Christian Science Monitor* (www.csmonitor.com), a prestigious online newspaper (Mon–Fri) and weekly print magazine, is published in Boston and is strong on international news.

Free weekly papers like the *Weekly Dig* (https://digboston.com) offer good features, well-written arts and music sections, and full city events listings. There is also the *Improper Bostonian* (www.improper.com), a free weekly lifestyle magazine. These can generally be found in sidewalk dispensers but the locations have dwindled in recent years. The information is also available on their websites.

In shops you can buy *Boston Magazine* (www.bostonmagazine.com), a slick, informative monthly magazine with local features and interviews. **Out of Town News** (tel: 617-354-1441) is a kiosk in the middle of Harvard Square that sells a range of national and international publications.

Radio: Stations include WBZ (http://boston.cbslocal.com) on 1030AM for news; WRKO (www.wrko.com) on 680AM for talk; WZLX digital station for rock music; and WGBH (www.wgbh.org) public radio on 89.7FM for national programs and 99.5FM for classical music.

Television: Stations include Channel 2 (www.wgbh.org) for public television; and the national networks CBS on Channel 4 WBZ (http://boston.cbslocal.com), ABC on Channel 5 WCVB (www.wcvb.com), NBC on Channel 7 WHDH (www1.whdh.com), and Fox on Channel 25 WFXT (www.myfoxboston.com).

Money

Major credit and debit cards are widely accepted. Some smaller restaurants accept cash only; they will usually post it in the menu, or you can check with your waiter beforehand. Car rental agencies and some hotels will require you to have a credit card. ATMs are plentiful.

Traveler's checks are easily converted to cash at any bank, but you will need your passport to prove your identity. Foreign currency exchange is not handled by all banks; your best bet for this is to head to a travel services companies.

Travelex, 745 Boylston Street, Boston; www.travelex.com.

American Express Travel, 1 State Street, Boston; tel: 617-723-8400; 39 J.F. Kennedy Street, Cambridge; tel: 617-868-2600.

P

Postal services

The main Post Office can be found at 25 Dorchester Avenue (behind South Station; tel: 617-654-5302; www.usps.gov; retail: Mon–Sat 6am–11.59pm, Sun 9am–5pm; limited lobby services: 24 hours). There are many branches across the city, most open Mon–Fri 9am–5pm, including at Logan Airport. Stamps are available in vending machines in airports, hotels, stores, bus and train stations, as well as online.

Public holidays

All government offices, banks, and post offices close on public holidays. Public transportation does not run as often on these days, but most shops, museums, and other attractions will be open.

Jan 1: New Year's Day
Third Mon Jan: Martin Luther King Day
Third Mon Feb: President's Day
March/April: Easter Sunday
Third Mon Apr: Patriot's Day
Last Mon May: Memorial Day
July 4: Independence Day
First Mon Sept: Labor Day
Second Mon Oct: Columbus Day
Last Thur and Fri Nov: Thanksgiving
Dec 25: Christmas

S

Smoking

Smoking is banned in all indoor public places across the state, including bars, clubs, and restaurants. In some bars there are outdoor areas set aside for smoking; if not, you have to go out on the street.

T

Taxes

All purchases, except unprepared food and clothing less than $175 per item, are subject to 6.25 per cent state sales tax. Clothing over $175 is taxed on the excess amount. Accessories (including shoes and bags) are subject to the tax.

Telephones

Phone numbers: All telephone numbers have ten digits. The Greater Boston area code, included in the number even when calling within the city, is 617. Surrounding towns use 857 (Brookline & Newton), 508 (Plymouth and Province-town), 781 & 339 (Lexington and Concord), 978 & 351 (Salem and Cape Ann) and 414 (Amherst and Deerfield). If you are calling outside the local area then a 1 precedes the 10-digit number.

Calling from abroad: To dial Boston from the UK: 00 (international code) + 1 (USA) + a 10-digit number. For calls to other countries from Boston dial the international access code (011), then the country code, city code, and local number. Directory assistance is 555-1212 preceded by 1 and the area code you are calling from or inquiring about; so for Boston call 1-617-555-1212.

Cell phones: Newer cell handsets from Europe and Asia work in US cities, but reception in suburban and rural areas tends to be spotty. This is improving as the US upgrades its cell infrastructure. Pay-as-you-go SIMs that will work in your phone, depending on the model, can purchased from several outlets throughout the city. Main companies are AT&T (www.att.com), Sprint (www.sprint.com), and Verizon (www.verizon.com).

Public telephone boxes: The popularity of cell (mobile) phones means you will find few public telephone booths in Boston.

Time zones

Boston is on Eastern Standard Time, which is five hours behind Greenwich Mean Time. The US has four time zones, so Boston is three hours ahead of Los Angeles, two hours ahead of Denver and one hour ahead of Chicago.

Tipping

Tipping is voluntary, but unlike in Europe service charges are not added to bills. Waiters, taxi drivers, bartenders, etc will expect gratuities, as this supplements their minimum wage pay. The standard amount is 15 per cent of the bill, with 20 per cent for above-average service and at better restaurants. Doormen, sky-cabs, and porters receive $1–2 per bag, and chambermaids, $1–3 per night.

Toilets

Public toilets in Boston are scarce. You can find listings for available facilities online (www.universalhub.com/restrooms). The best options are libraries, hotel lobbies, shopping malls or asking politely at a restaurant or café.

Tourist information

The **Greater Boston Convention and Visitors Bureau** (Two Copley Place; tel: 617-536-4100/1-888-733-2678; www.bostonusa.com) runs two visitor centers:

Boston Common Visitor Information Center, 148 Tremont Street; Mon–Fri 8.30am–5pm, Sat–Sun 9am–5pm (the booth here marks the start of the Freedom Trail).

Prudential Visitor Center, Center Court, Prudential Center, 800 Boylston Street; Mon–Fri 9am–5.30pm, Sat–Sun 10am–6pm.

The Cambridge Office of Tourism (4 Brattle Street, Cambridge; tel: 1-800-862-5678/617-441-2884; www.cambridge-usa.org) has a booth in the center of Harvard Square (tel: 617-497-1630; Mon–Fri 9am–5pm, Sat–Sun 9am–1pm).

Massachusetts Office of Travel and Tourism, 10 Park Plaza, Suite 4510; tel: 617-973-8500; www.massvacation.com. Supplies information on Boston and the state.

Massport International Information Booth, Logan International Airport (Terminal E); summer noon–8pm; winter noon–6pm.

There are two **National Park Service Visitor Centers** (www.nps.gov/bost), both open daily 9am to 5pm: Charlestown Navy Yard (tel: 617-242-5601), and Faneuil Hall (tel: 617-242-5642).

Transportation

Arrival by air

Logan Airport (tel: 1-800-235-6426; www.massport.com) has four terminals (A–C and E). Airlines do not necessarily use the same terminal for domestic and international flights. There are free shuttle buses that are wheelchair-lift-equipped and run between the terminals. In addition, an on-call (tel: 617-561-1770) lift-equipped van serves all Logan Airport's facilities; it can be requested from any Public Information Booth at the arrivals level/baggage claim.

From the airport

Logan is only 3 miles (4.8km) from Downtown Boston. **Logan Shuttle**

buses (www.massport.com) connect the terminals' arrival levels with the MBTA Blue Line (T-stop: Airport; tel: 617-222-3200; www.mbta.com). It takes about 10 minutes to Downtown, where you can transfer to the Green Line (T-stop: Government Center) and Orange Line (T-stop: State Street).

The **Silver Line** is a rapid-transit bus service, also part of the MBTA system, which stops at all the airport terminals and connects with the Red Line and Amtrak train (T-stop: South Station), before continuing to the South End.

Taxis are stationed outside each terminal. Fares to the city or to Cambridge are approximately $30–$40 (excluding tip and surcharges) providing there are no major traffic jams. A surcharge that covers the tolls ($5.25) and airport fees ($2.25) is added to any trips going into the city. Also see the Massport website for details of flat fares to suburban areas.

Ridesharing services such as Uber and Lyft are now able to pick up and drop off at the airport. On collections they may need to wait in the parking areas.

Water shuttles are a delightful way to approach the city, and convenient if you are staying in Downtown, North End, or the Waterfront. Operators include:

   City Water Taxi (tel: 617-227-4320; www.bostonharborcruises.com; Mon–Sat 7am–10pm, Sun 7am–8pm; $12 one-way). Private service to around 30 landings in Boston Harbor.

Rowes Wharf Water Transport (tel: 617-406-8584; www.roweswharf-watertransport.com; Nov–Apr daily 7am–7pm, April–Nov until 10pm; $12 one-way, $20 round trip). Private service to 30 locations in the harbor.

Arrival by land

By rail: South Station (Atlantic Avenue and Summer Street) is the east coast terminus for Amtrak (tel: 1-800-872-7245/1, TDD/TTY 1-800-523-6590, 800-033-7810 (in UK only); www. amtrak.com). Passengers can travel on northbound trains from Washington, DC, New York, and Philadelphia, with connections from all points in the nationwide Amtrak system. In addition, daily trains arrive from Chicago to Boston by way of Cleveland, Buffalo, Rochester, and Albany NY. Prior to arriving at South Station, the train stops at Back Bay Station (145 Dartmouth Street), which is convenient for access to Back Bay and the South End.

By bus: Several intercity bus companies serve Boston. The two largest, Greyhound (tel: 1-800-231-2222; www.greyhound.com) and **Peter Pan** (tel: 1-800-343-9999; www.peter panbus.com), have daily services to almost anywhere in the US. Services to Cape Cod are provided by **Plymouth & Brockton** (tel: 508-746-0378; www.p-b.com). All buses leave from the bus terminal next to South Station.

By car: Free up-to-date traffic information is available by dialing 511 on your cell phone.

From the west: the Massachusetts Turnpike (Mass Pike or I-90) toll road is the best route into town from the west. Take Exit 18 Cambridge/Allston for Cambridge and Harvard Square; Exit 22 Prudential Center/Copley Square for Back Bay, Fenway, Kenmore Square, and Boston Common; Exit 24 for Downtown and access to Route 93.

From the south: Routes 95, 24 and 3 all feed into Route 1 which turns into Route 93 North; Exit 20 (South Station/I-90) is best for Downtown; Exit 23 (Government Center) for Waterfront, and Exit 26 (Storrow Drive) is best for Beacon Hill and Back Bay.

From the north: Routes 95, 1 and 93 enter Boston on elevated highway structures; Exit 26 (Storrow Drive) is best for Beacon Hill and Back Bay; Exit 23B-A (Government Center) is best for North End and Downtown; 20B-A (South Station) is best for Waterfront.

Transportation within Boston

LinkPass: A cost-effective way for visitors to use the MBTA system is the LinkPass. It allows unlimited use of the subway, buses, and water shuttles, plus Zone 1A of the commuter rail lines, for one ($12) or seven days ($21.25), or one month ($84.50). LinkPass cards can be purchased at almost all stations. Monthly LinkPasses are valid only on subways and buses.

Subway: MBTA (tel: 617-222-3200/1-800-392-6100; www.mbta.com; Mon–Sat 5am–1am, Sun 5.40am–1am) operates the oldest subway in the US. Carriages can get crowded during the rush hours, but it is generally efficient and user-friendly. The four main lines – Red, Green, Orange, and Blue – radiate out from Downtown where the lines intersect; riders can transfer between the lines at no charge. Two Silver Line routes are shown on subway maps, but these are both bus services and charge bus rather than subway fares.

If you need transfer to a bus (also run by the MBTA) you can ask for a transfer at the ticket booth. 'Inbound' means toward Downtown – Park Street, Downtown Crossing, State Street, and Government Center. 'Outbound' means away from Downtown. All four lines have branches that extend beyond central Boston. Check the destination on the front of the trains. Last trains leave Downtown around 12.45am; there are minor differences in the last trains between the lines, so check postings in the station.

To use the subway purchase a Charlie Ticket ($2.75) from a station machine. A single ticket permits travel on the entire 'Outbound' length of a line, but there is an 'Inbound' surcharge on extensions of the Green Line. If you board the T at surface stations where there is no ticket machine, you will need the exact fare, as conductors do not carry change. The

Charlie Card (www.mbta.com/fares_ and_passes/charlie) is a plastic stored-value card. If you use this then each ride is $2.25, and you can get free transfers to MBTA buses (not possible with the Charlie Tickets). Accompanied children under 11 travel free.

Buses: Few of MBTA's 160-plus bus routes enter Downtown, and most of these are express services from outlying areas. Route 1 travels along Massachusetts Avenue (from Back Bay) across the Charles River to MIT and on to Harvard Square. Single rides are $2 or $1.50 using a Charlie Card. Express buses are $4.00–7.00. Transfers to the subway are discounted only if you are using a Charlie Card. If you do not have the exact fare you will be given change in the form of a Charlie Ticket.

Commuter Rail: The MBTA Commuter Rail (tel: 1-800-392-6100) extends from downtown Boston to as far as 60 miles (almost 100km) away, serving such tourist destinations as Concord and Salem. Trains to the north and the northwest of Boston depart from North Station (135 Causeway Street), while trains to points south and west leave from South Station (Atlantic Avenue and Summer Street). Most south-side commuter trains also stop at Back Bay Station.

Taxis: Boston has plenty of taxis, although on a rainy day this seems barely credible. There are also taxi lines at most hotels and highly trafficked areas. Note that Boston taxis are not allowed to pick up in Cambridge and vice versa. All tolls are paid for by the passenger, and there is no charge for extra passengers, but the driver may add a charge for heavy suitcases. For trips over 12 miles (20km) from Downtown there are flat rates.

The following taxi companies take phone bookings:

Boston:
Boston Cab, tel: 617-536-5010; www. bostoncab.us
Metro Cab, tel: 617-782-5500; http:// boston-cab.com
Town Taxi, tel: 617-536-5000; www. towntaxiboston.com

Cambridge:
Cabbie's Cab, tel: 617-547-2222; www.cabbiescab.com

Driving and car rental
Drivers must be aged 21 or above to rent, and rates may be higher if you are under 25. Child seats are available for an additional cost and are compulsory for children under five or under 40lbs (18kg). The speed limit on Interstate highways is 55–65mph (88–104kmh); in the city and surrounding communities it is 20–30mph (35–45kmh). Right turns at a red traffic signal are permitted unless there is a NO TURN ON RED sign. On entering a roundabout (rotary), you must yield to vehicles already in it.

All the major car rental companies have outlets at the airport.
Avis, tel: 617-561-3500; www.avis.com

Traffic in Back Bay

Budget, tel: 617-497-3733; www.budget.com

Dollar Rent A Car, tel: 617-634-0006; www.dollar.com

Enterprise, tel: 617-561-4488; www.enterprise.com

Hertz, tel: 617-569-7272; www.hertz.com

National, tel: 1-888-826-6890; www.nationalcar.com

Thrifty, tel: 1-877-283-0898; www.thrifty.com

Bicycle rental

Boston has plenty of dedicated trails that are good for both cyclist and in-line skaters. BLUEbikes (www.bluebikes.com) is a new bike sharing system offering around 1,100 bikes at 112 locations across the city. A variety of pricing options includes rates as low as $2.50 for a single ride. Bikes may be rented from:

Community Bicycle Supply, 496 Tremont Street; tel: 617-542-8623; www.communitybicycle.com; Apr–Sept Mon–Fri 10am–7pm, Sat 10am–6pm, Sun noon–5pm, Oct–Mar, Mon–Sat 10am–6pm, Wed and Fri until 7pm.

Urban Adventours; 103 Atlantic Avenue; tel: 617-670-0637; www.urbanadventours.com; bike rental (from $35 a day) and tours.

V

Visas

Immigration into the US is handled by the US Citizenship and Immigration Service (tel: 1-800-767-1833; www.uscis.gov). Visitors must have a valid passport, visa, or other accepted documentation. The US offers the Visa Waiver Program for those coming on vacation for a maximum of 90 days. With 37 countries participating, the program allows for select travelers to enter the US with only a machine readable passport. Recent increased security now requires all VWP participants to apply with the Electronic System for Travel Authorization online. You need to do this at least 72 hours before travel and there is an administration fee of $14. The rules are continually evolving, so check USCIS before you set off (tel: 202-663-1225; www.state.gov).

W

Websites

www.bostonusa.com Greater Boston Convention and Visitors Bureau's official site.

www.massvacation.com Massachusetts Office of Travel and Tourism's site provides information for the entire state.

www.mbta.com For up-to-date information about the transportation system.

www.massport.com All you need to know about Logan Airport.

www.capecodchamber.org Cape Cod Chamber of Commerce information.

www.visitNewEngland.com Information about the region.

www.northofboston.org Details of places to the north of the city.

The 'Make Way for Ducklings' sculpture in the Public Garden

BOOKS AND FILM

Boston's past and present are defined by its literary culture. Boston was where the first book in America, the *Bay Psalm Book*, was published, and where literary greats like Emerson, Thoreau, and Whitman explored the connection between Boston's beautiful surroundings and the innermost workings of the soul. Its network of universities has provided fertile ground for literary minds and culture for centuries, and many of America's current bestselling authors continue to draw on Boston's rich literary history for inspiration.

The city has also become a popular filming destination thanks to its city government, which has lured film companies away from popular settings like New York City and Los Angeles with lowered restrictions and tax breaks. Films have long been fascinated with the contradictions in Boston's cityscape. The notorious gangs of South Boston and Charlestown, and the legacy of its tough Irish immigrant past are often contrasted with the calm gentility of the Beacon Hill and Back Bay neighborhoods and the hallowed halls of Harvard University and MIT.

Books

Non-fiction
About Boston, by David McCord. Boston's essence distilled into short, poetic chapters, written by a poet and educator who was honored by the city with the title Grand Bostonian. First published in 1948.

Boston: A Topographical History, Third Enlarged Edition by Walter Muir Whitehall, and enlarged by Lawrence Kennedy. A vivid historical survey of Boston with a focus on physical changes, illustrated with old pictures and maps. First published in 1968.

Cityscapes of Boston, by Robert Campbell and Peter Vanderwarker. A Boston historical survey, beautifully illustrated with black-and-white images comparing sites in the past and present.

The Houses of Boston's Back Bay, by Bainbridge Bunting. Seminal, immensely detailed review of Back Bay architecture.

The Islands of Boston Harbor, by Edward Rowe Snow, updated by Jeremy D'Entremont. History and legends of the Harbor Islands.

Lost Boston, by Jane Holtz Kay. A classic architectural history of Boston which is handsomely illustrated.

Paul Revere and the World He Lived In, by Esther Forbes. Pulitzer Prize-winning account of Revere's life and the American Revolution.

The Proper Bostonians, by Cleveland Amory. Some very entertaining insights into the city's social framework.

Fiction
On Beauty, by Zadie Smith. Follows a mixed-race British/American family liv-

Leonardo DiCaprio in 'The Departed'

ing in a fictional town outside Boston.

The Bostonians, by Henry James. A 19th-century satire of the city's radical and reformist circles.

The Friends of Eddie Coyle, by George Higgins. Part of a Boston-based series; other titles include *Cogan's Trade*, *Impostors*, *Outlaws*, *Penance for Jerry Kennedy*.

The Last Puritan, by George Santayana. The life of Puritan Oliver Alden, conflicted over his sense of duty and natural instincts.

The Late George Apley, by John P. Marquand. A 1937 satire of Boston upper-class society.

Little Women, by Louisa May Alcott. Four sisters – Meg, Jo, Beth and Amy March – grow up in 19th-century New England.

The Rise of Silas Lapham, by William Dean Howells. Rags-to-riches story, and accompanying moral dilemmas.

The Scarlet Letter, by Nathaniel Hawthorne. Adulteress Hester Pyrne struggles for repentance in 17th-century Puritan Boston.

For children

Make Way for Ducklings, by Robert McCloskey. A family of ducks live in the Boston Public Garden's Lagoon.

The Trumpet of the Swan, by E.B. White. Story of a trumpeter swan born without a voice that learns to play the trumpet.

Films

Good Will Hunting (1997). This Oscar-winning movie made stars of then-unknown actors and writers Matt Damon and Ben Affleck. When Will Hunting, a janitor at MIT, solves an equation that stumps the university's brightest stars, he garners the notice of its top math professor – and a psychologist (Robin Williams).

Mystic River (2003). This dark film, directed by Clint Eastwood, tells the story of Dave, Jimmy and Sean, three working-class Bostonians whose lives are shaped by the memory of a shared childhood tragedy. Features an all-star cast (Sean Penn, Tim Robbins, Kevin Bacon).

The Departed (2006). Matt Damon and Leonardo DiCaprio play two spies in the war between the Massachusetts Police Department and Boston's notorious Irish mob, led by Francis 'Frank' Costello (Jack Nicholson). Directed by Martin Scorsese (who finally won a Best Director Oscar), the movie was adapted from 2002's *Infernal Affairs*.

The Town (2010). Ben Affleck returns to his hometown to direct and star in this well-received movie. As he plans his next job, a thief tries to balance his feelings for a bank manager connected to one of his earlier heists. Also starring Rebecca Hall, Jeremy Renner, and Jon Hamm.

Spotlight (2015). The biographical drama starring Mark Ruffalo tells the story of the investigative journalists working for the Boston Globe who uncovered the Catholic Church sexual abuse scandal in Boston. The movie won Best Picture and Best Original Screenplay at the 88th Academy Awards.

ABOUT THIS BOOK

This *Explore Guide* has been produced by the editors of Insight Guides, whose books have set the standard for visual travel guides since 1970. With top-quality photography and authoritative recommendations, these guidebooks bring you the very best routes and itineraries in the world's most exciting destinations.

BEST ROUTES

The routes in the book provide something to suit all budgets, tastes and trip lengths. As well as covering the destination's many classic attractions, the itineraries track lesser-known sights, and there are also excursions for those who want to extend their visit outside the city. The routes embrace a range of interests, so whether you are an art fan, a gourmet, a history buff or have kids to entertain, you will find an option to suit.

We recommend reading the whole of a route before setting out. This should help you to familiarise yourself with it and enable you to plan where to stop for refreshments – options are shown in the 'Food and drink' box at the end of each tour.

For our pick of the tours by theme, consult Recommended routes for… (see pages 6–7).

INTRODUCTION

The routes are set in context by this introductory section, giving an overview of the destination to set the scene, plus background information on food and drink, shopping and more, while a succinct history timeline highlights the key events over the centuries.

DIRECTORY

Also supporting the routes is a Directory chapter, with a clearly organised A–Z of practical information, our pick of where to stay while you are there and select restaurant listings; these eateries complement the more low-key cafés and restaurants that feature within the routes and are intended to offer a wider choice for evening dining. Also included here are some nightlife listings and our recommendations for books and films about the destination.

ABOUT THE AUTHORS

During his career as a journalist and photographer, award-winning travel writer Simon Richmond has lived in several cities, including London, Tokyo, Sydney and Boston. He has authored and contributed to over 30 different travel guidebooks from Cape Town to the Trans-Siberian Railway, as well as restaurant and activity guides; he has worked for Insight Guides on guides to Tokyo and New England. Compact, historic, but also modern, Boston is, in Simon's view, one of the best cities to discover on foot. This book builds on work by travel writer Marcus Brooke, who used to teach at Harvard and MIT. Thanks also go to Anna Nieniewska, Jackie Staddon, and Hilary Weston.

CONTACT THE EDITORS

We hope you find this Explore Guide useful, interesting and a pleasure to read. If you have any questions or feedback on the text, pictures or maps, please do let us know. If you have noticed any errors or outdated facts, or have suggestions for places to include on the routes, we would be delighted to hear from you. Please drop us an email at hello@insightguides.com. Thanks!

CREDITS

917.4461   (111)
INS
2018

Explore Boston

Second Edition 2018

Editor: Sian Marsh
Author: Simon Richmond
Head of DTP and Pre-Press: Rebeka Davies
Update Production: Apa Digital
Picture Editor: Tom Smyth
Cartography: original cartography
Berndston & Berndston, updated by Carte
Photo credits: Abraham Nowitz/Apa
Publications 4MR, 4MC, 6MC, 7MR, 8ML,
8MR, 8/9T, 23, 24MR, 24MR, 26, 30, 33L,
35L, 36, 37, 38, 41, 44, 45L, 44/45, 50,
54, 61, 66, 76/77, 78, 79L, 82, 83L, 84,
89L, 98MC, 98MR, 98MC, 103, 114, 126,
130/131, 132/133, 134/135; Alamy 137;
bigstock 136; Dreamstime 11, 32/33,
42/43, 70/71, 72/73; Fotolia 60; Getty
Images 20, 21, 112, 113, 116; iStock 1,
4/5T, 8ML, 10, 12, 16, 24/25T, 28, 34/35,
46, 46/47, 78/79, 86, 87, 91, 92, 94, 95,
97, 102; Jorge Hernández Cultural Center
71L; Leonardo 100, 101, 106, 106/107,
107L, 108/109, 117, 118/119, 120, 122;
Mark Read/Apa Publications 68, 69L, 96;
Mary Evans Picture Library 22; Rex Features
70; Richard Nowitz/Apa Publications 4ML,
4MC, 4MR, 4ML, 6TL, 6ML, 6BC, 7T, 7MR,
7M, 8MC, 8MC, 8MR, 13, 14/15, 16/17,
17L, 18, 18/19, 19L, 24ML, 24MC, 24ML,
24MC, 27L, 26/27, 29L, 28/29, 30/31, 31L,
32, 34, 39, 40, 47L, 48/49, 50/51, 51L, 52,
53, 55L, 54/55, 56, 57, 58, 59, 62, 63, 64,
64/65, 65L, 67, 68/69, 74, 74/75, 76, 77L,
80, 80/81, 81L, 82/83, 84/85, 85L, 88,
88/89, 90, 92/93, 93L, 98ML, 98MR, 98ML,
98/99T, 104/105, 110/111, 121, 123,
124/125, 127, 128/129; Starwood Hotels &
Resorts 115
Cover credits: iStock (main & bottom)

Printed by CTPS – China

DISTRIBUTION

UK, Ireland and Europe
Apa Publications (UK) Ltd
sales@insightguides.com
United States and Canada
Ingram Publisher Services
ips@ingramcontent.com
Australia and New Zealand
Woodslane
info@woodslane.com.au
Southeast Asia
Apa Publications (Singapore) Pte
singaporeoffice@insightguides.com
Worldwide
Apa Publications (UK) Ltd
sales@insightguides.com

SPECIAL SALES, CONTENT LICENSING AND COPUBLISHING

Insight Guides can be purchased in bulk
quantities at discounted prices. We can
create special editions, personalised jackets
and corporate imprints tailored to your needs.
sales@insightguides.com
www.insightguides.biz

INDEX

MAP LEGEND

● Start of tour

→ Tour & route direction

❶ Recommended sight

❷ Recommended restaurant/café

★ Place of interest

ⓘ Tourist information

Ⓣ Subway station

🗿 Statue/monument

✉ Main post office

🚌 Main bus station

--- Ferry route

Park

Important building

Hotel

Transport hub

Shop / market

Pedestrian area

Urban area

INSIGHT ⊙ GUIDES
OFF THE SHELF

Since 1970, INSIGHT GUIDES has provided a unique perspective on the world's best travel destinations by using specially commissioned photography and illuminating text written by local authors.

Whether you're planning a city break, a walking tour or the journey of a lifetime, our superb range of guidebooks and phrasebooks will inspire you to discover more about your chosen destination.

INSIGHT GUIDES

offer a unique combination of stunning photos, absorbing narrative and detailed maps, providing all the inspiration and information you need.

PHRASEBOOKS & DICTIONARIES

help users to feel at home, when away. Pocket-sized with a free app to download, they go where you do.

CITY GUIDES

pack hundreds of great photos into a smaller format with detailed practical information, so you can navigate the world's top cities with confidence.

EXPLORE GUIDES

feature easy-to-follow walks and itineraries in the world's most exciting destinations, with our choice of the best places to eat and drink along the way.

POCKET GUIDES

combine concise information on where to go and what to do in a handy compact format, ideal on the ground. Includes a full-colour, fold-out map.

EXPERIENCE GUIDES

feature offbeat perspectives and secret gems for experienced travellers, with a collection of over 100 ideas for a memorable stay in a city.

www.insightguides.com